Building Go Apps, Essential Tips and Tricks for Developing with Go Language

Learn the Best Practices for Efficient, Scalable Software with Go

Booker Blunt

Rafael Sanders

Miguel Farmer

Boozman Richard

Contents

[4]

Contents

[14]

How to Scan a Barcode to Get a Repository

1. **Install a QR/Barcode Scanner** – Ensure you have a barcode or QR code scanner app installed on your smartphone or use a built-in scanner in **GitHub, GitLab, or Bitbucket.**

2. **Open the Scanner** – Launch the scanner app and grant necessary camera permissions.

3. **Scan the Barcode** – Align the barcode within the scanning frame. The scanner will automatically detect and process it.

4. **Follow the Link** – The scanned result will display a **URL to the repository.** Tap the link to open it in your web browser or Git client.

5. **Clone the Repository** – Use **Git clone** with the provided URL to download the repository to your local machine.

Introduction to Go for Software Development

1. Introduction

In the world of software development, the number of programming languages is overwhelming. From JavaScript to Python, Java to Ruby, the choices can be daunting. However, in recent years, **Go** (also known as **Golang**) has emerged as one of the most popular and powerful languages for building scalable and efficient applications, particularly in the realms of backend development, microservices, and cloud computing.

But why is Go gaining so much traction among developers, and why should you care about learning it?

The answer lies in Go's unique combination of simplicity, speed, and scalability. It offers an elegant approach to solving problems that other languages struggle with. Whether you're a **beginner** trying to make your way into software development or a **seasoned professional** looking to improve your skills, **Go** offers a set of features that simplify complex development tasks and make writing robust applications quicker and more efficient.

In this chapter, we will explore **why Go stands out**, the **core concepts** that make it unique, and how this book can help you master the language. Along the way, we will cover **real-world** examples, **hands-on tutorials,** and **practical projects** that will set you on the path to building your own Go applications.

Go's Rise in Popularity

Go was developed by **Google** in 2007 and released as an open-source language in 2009. Its primary goal was to create a language that addressed the challenges of developing software at scale, particularly in environments requiring high-performance and concurrent programming. Today, Go is widely used in companies such as **Uber, Dropbox, Netflix,** and **Docker,** and is a favorite for building everything from web servers to data pipelines.

Whether you're working on small applications or building distributed systems, Go provides a smooth experience with its lightweight and fast execution. It has become synonymous with **cloud-native** applications, making it a **must-learn** language for developers in modern software ecosystems.

In this chapter, we will explore:

- Why you should choose Go for software development

- What makes Go stand out from other programming languages

- How this book will guide you to build real-world applications with Go

2. Core Concepts and Theory

To truly appreciate why Go is the language of choice for many developers, it's essential to understand the **core concepts** that make it stand out. In this section, we'll explore the fundamental building blocks of Go that set it apart from other programming languages.

Go's Simplicity and Readability

One of the core strengths of Go is its simplicity. The language was designed to be easy to learn and use, while still being powerful enough to handle complex software development needs. Go's syntax is **minimalist** and avoids unnecessary features, which can often lead to code bloat in other languages.

Analogy: Think of Go as a high-performance vehicle—everything in its design serves a purpose, ensuring efficiency and speed, without unnecessary add-ons that slow it down.

Here's an example of Go's simplicity:

```go
package main

import "fmt"

func main() {
    fmt.Println("Hello, Go!")
}
```

This is a basic Go program that prints a message to the console. Notice how the code is straightforward: no complex syntax, no boilerplate, just the essentials. This is what makes Go so appealing to both beginners and experienced developers—less clutter, more focus on solving problems.

Go's Strong Concurrency Model

Another key feature that sets Go apart is its **concurrency model**, which allows developers to build applications that can perform multiple tasks simultaneously. Go's concurrency is based on the concept of **goroutines** and **channels**.

- **Goroutines:** Lightweight threads that allow you to run functions concurrently without the overhead of traditional threads.

- **Channels:** A way to communicate between goroutines, enabling them to synchronize and share data safely.

This model makes Go ideal for applications that need to handle high concurrency, such as web servers or real-time applications.

Example: Here's an example of using goroutines and channels in Go:

```go

package main

import "fmt"

func greet(name string, ch chan string) {
    ch <- "Hello, " + name
```

```
}

func main() {
    ch := make(chan string)
    go greet("Go Programmer", ch)
    fmt.Println(<-ch)
}
```

In this example:

- We create a goroutine that runs the greet function.

- We use a **channel** to send the greeting back to the main function.

- The main function prints the result once it receives the message.

This code demonstrates how Go makes concurrent programming simple and efficient.

Go's Garbage Collection

Go handles **memory management** automatically with its built-in **garbage collector**. This allows developers to focus on writing code without worrying about manual memory management, which is often error-prone and tedious in other languages.

The Go garbage collector runs in the background and automatically reclaims unused memory, which enhances the performance and stability of applications.

Go's Static Typing and Interfaces

Go is a **statistically typed** language, meaning the type of every variable is known at compile time. This leads to **fewer runtime errors** and helps catch bugs early. Go also supports **interfaces**, which are a key part of its object-oriented nature, allowing for flexible and reusable code.

Analogy: Think of Go's type system as a well-organized toolset, where each tool (or variable) has a designated place. This keeps everything structured and reduces confusion, especially in large applications.

Go's Package System and Modular Code

Go promotes **modularity** and **reusability** through its **package system**. By organizing code into distinct packages, developers can easily manage and scale applications. Go's package system encourages **separation of concerns**, which makes code more maintainable and testable.

3. Tools and Setup

Before diving into hands-on projects, it's crucial to set up your development environment properly. In this section, we'll guide you through the **tools** and **platforms** you'll need to start coding with Go. We'll also provide clear, step-by-step instructions for setting up your environment.

Installing Go

First, you need to install Go on your machine. The installation process is straightforward, and Go provides excellent documentation to guide you through it.

Step 1: Download Go

Go to the official Go website and download the latest stable version for your operating system.

Step 2: Install Go

Follow the instructions for your operating system. For **Windows**, the installer will guide you through the setup process. On **macOS** and **Linux**, you'll typically use a package manager like Homebrew or APT.

Step 3: Verify Installation

Once installed, open your terminal and type:

```bash
```

```
go version
```

This will display the installed Go version, confirming the installation is successful.

Setting Up Your Go Workspace

Go relies on a **workspace** where all your Go code is stored. The workspace typically consists of three directories:

- **src/**: Contains the source code.

- **pkg/**: Contains compiled package files.

- **bin/**: Contains executable files.

To set up your workspace:

1. Create a folder called go in your home directory.

2. Inside go, create the three directories (src, pkg, bin).

After that, you'll need to set the GOPATH environment variable to point to your workspace:

```bash
export GOPATH=$HOME/go
```

Go IDE and Text Editors

Go can be written in any text editor, but using an integrated development environment (IDE) or a text editor with Go support will enhance your productivity. Popular editors include:

- **Visual Studio Code** (VS Code) with the Go plugin.

- **GoLand**, a specialized IDE for Go development.

- **Sublime Text** or **Atom** with Go packages.

Each of these editors provides **syntax highlighting**, **auto-completion**, and **debugging tools** to help you write Go code more efficiently.

Running Your First Go Program

Once your environment is set up, it's time to write your first Go program! Follow these steps:

1. Create a file called main.go inside the src directory.

2. Open the file and write a simple program:

```go
package main

import "fmt"

func main() {
    fmt.Println("Hello, Go!")
}
```

3. Save the file and run it from the terminal:

```bash
go run main.go
```

This will compile and execute the program, displaying Hello, Go! in the terminal.

---

4. Hands-on Examples & Projects

Now that your environment is set up and you have a basic understanding of Go's core concepts, let's dive into some hands-on projects that will help you apply what you've learned.

Project 1: Building a Simple Calculator

We'll start by building a simple calculator that can handle basic arithmetic operations like addition, subtraction, multiplication, and division. This project will reinforce the concepts of functions, control flow, and user input.

Project 2: Building a RESTful API for a To-Do List

In this project, we'll build a simple REST API for a to-do list application. This will introduce you to **HTTP servers, routes,** and **JSON handling** in Go.

Project 3: Concurrency with Goroutines and Channels

Next, we'll build a **concurrent downloader** that can download multiple files simultaneously using Go's **goroutines** and **channels**. This project will give you hands-on experience with Go's concurrency model.

Project 4: Web Scraping with Go

We will create a web scraper that fetches data from a website and extracts useful information. This will introduce you to **HTTP requests** and **parsing HTML** in Go.

5. Advanced Techniques & Optimization

In this section, we'll explore **advanced Go techniques**, including optimizing code for performance, leveraging Go's **profiling tools**, and handling **large-scale applications**. These tips are aimed at experienced developers looking to get the most out of Go.

6. Troubleshooting and Problem-Solving

Here, we'll cover common challenges and mistakes that Go developers face. We'll also provide practical tips for **debugging** and **troubleshooting** your Go applications.

7. Conclusion & Next Steps

We've covered the essentials of Go in this chapter—from the core concepts and setup to practical examples and advanced techniques. In the next chapters, we will dive deeper into building real-world applications with Go.

Next steps: Keep practicing by building projects, explore more advanced topics, and continue learning through online resources and communities.

Chapter 1: Getting Started with Go

Introduction

Welcome to the world of Go programming! If you're new to programming or looking to expand your knowledge, this chapter is your starting point in learning how to work with **Go**, one of the most powerful and efficient programming languages of today. Whether you're a beginner, hobbyist, or professional developer, Go (also known as **Golang**) offers you a simple yet robust platform to develop a wide range of applications—from web servers and cloud services to distributed systems.

So, why should you consider learning Go?

Go was developed by **Google** in 2007 and released as an open-source language in 2009. Its design emphasizes simplicity, efficiency, and scalability, making it ideal for building high-performance applications. It's fast, has excellent support for concurrency (handling multiple tasks simultaneously), and is easy to deploy.

The goal of this chapter is to help you **get started** with Go and provide you with the essential knowledge needed to begin writing Go programs. We will explore the steps involved in setting up Go on your machine, understanding its syntax and structure, writing your first simple program, and getting familiar with Go modules and packages.

Why Learn Go?

Go has seen tremendous growth in recent years, with companies like **Netflix**, **Uber**, and **Dropbox** adopting it for building scalable backend systems. As a beginner, you'll find that Go is one of the best languages for learning software development due to its simplicity and powerful features.

Key features of Go:

- **Simplicity:** Go's syntax is clean and easy to read, making it ideal for beginners.

- **Concurrency support:** Go offers goroutines and channels, making concurrent programming simple and efficient.

- **Performance:** Go is a statically typed, compiled language, which means it runs quickly and efficiently.

- **Built-in memory management:** Go comes with garbage collection, so you don't need to manually manage memory allocation and deallocation.

By the end of this chapter, you'll have installed Go on your machine, written your first program, and learned the fundamentals needed to start developing real-world applications in Go.

Core Concepts and Theory

Before diving into writing code, let's explore the core concepts that form the foundation of Go programming. By understanding Go's syntax, structure, and key features, you'll be able to write effective and efficient Go code.

Understanding Go's Syntax and Structure

Go has a relatively simple syntax, designed to be easy to read and write. Unlike many other programming languages, Go avoids unnecessary complexities and focuses on being practical. Here's a breakdown of the basic syntax you'll need to know:

1. Go Program Structure

A Go program consists of **packages**. Every Go program starts with the **main** package. Below is a simple Go program structure:

```go

package main

import "fmt" // Importing the fmt package
for formatted output

func main() { // Entry point for the program
    fmt.Println("Hello, Go!") // Print a
message to the console
}
```

- **package main:** Every executable Go program starts with the main package.

- **import:** Go uses packages to organize code. In this example, we import the fmt package, which provides formatted I/O functions like Println.

- **func main():** The main function is the starting point of execution in Go programs.

2. Variables and Data Types

In Go, variables are explicitly typed. Here are some basic data types:

- **int**: Integer type, used to represent whole numbers.
- **float64**: Floating-point numbers, used for decimal values.
- **string**: A sequence of characters.
- **bool**: Boolean values (true or false).

Here's an example of defining and using variables:

```go
package main

import "fmt"

func main() {
    var a int = 10
    var b float64 = 3.14
    var name string = "Go Developer"
    var isGoFun bool = true

    fmt.Println(a, b, name, isGoFun)
}
```

- The var keyword is used to declare variables.
- You can specify the type (e.g., int, float64) or let Go infer it.

3. Functions and Control Flow

Go is a **procedural language**, meaning that code is organized into functions. You can define functions with the func keyword.

Here's a function that returns the sum of two integers:

```go
package main

import "fmt"

func add(x int, y int) int {
    return x + y
}

func main() {
    result := add(5, 3)
    fmt.Println("Sum:", result)
}
```

- **Functions:** add(x int, y int) defines a function that takes two integers and returns their sum.

- **Control Flow:** Go includes standard control structures like if, else, for, switch, and defer for managing flow control.

Here's an example of an if statement in Go:

```go
package main

import "fmt"

func main() {
    x := 5
    if x > 3 {
        fmt.Println("x is greater than 3")
    }
}
```

Concurrency in Go: Goroutines and Channels

One of Go's standout features is its support for **concurrency**. Concurrency is the ability of a program to handle multiple tasks at the same time. Go achieves this through **goroutines** and **channels**.

1. Goroutines

A **goroutine** is a lightweight thread managed by the Go runtime. You can launch a goroutine by simply adding the go keyword before a function call:

```go
go

package main

import "fmt"

func greet(name string) {
    fmt.Println("Hello, ", name)
}

func main() {
    go greet("Go Programmer")
    fmt.Println("Main function running
concurrently!")
}
```

- **Concurrency with Goroutines**: In the code above, the greet function runs concurrently with the main function. Go automatically manages the scheduling of goroutines.

2. Channels

Go provides **channels** to communicate between goroutines. A channel allows one goroutine to send data to another.

Here's an example that demonstrates the use of a channel:

```go
package main

import "fmt"

func greet(name string, ch chan string) {
    ch <- "Hello, " + name
}

func main() {
    ch := make(chan string) // Create a new
channel
    go greet("Go Developer", ch)
    msg := <-ch // Receive a message from
the channel
    fmt.Println(msg)
}
```

- **Channel:** The ch variable is a channel of type string. The greet function sends a message to the channel, and the main function receives it.

Tools and Setup

Now that you have a fundamental understanding of Go's syntax and concurrency, it's time to set up your development environment and get started coding. Follow these steps to get Go up and running on your machine.

Step 1: Installing Go

To install Go, follow these instructions for your operating system:

- **Windows**: Download the installer from the Go Downloads page, run the installer, and follow the prompts.

- **macOS**: Use Homebrew or download the .pkg installer from the Go website.

- **Linux**: Use a package manager like apt or yum, or download the Go tarball from the Go website.

Once installed, verify that Go is properly installed by running:

bash

```
go version
```
This command will print the installed version of Go.

Step 2: Setting Up Your Go Workspace

Go uses a **workspace** where all your Go code is stored. It includes three main directories:

- **src/**: Contains source files.

- **pkg/**: Contains compiled package files.

- **bin/**: Contains executable files.

Create a workspace directory and set the GOPATH environment variable:

bash

```
export GOPATH=$HOME/go
export PATH=$PATH:$GOPATH/bin
```

Step 3: Using Go Modules

Go Modules is the official dependency management system in Go, introduced in version 1.11. It allows you to manage your project's dependencies.

To create a new Go project with modules:

1. Initialize the module in your project folder:

bash

```
go mod init myproject
```

2. Add dependencies by running:

bash

```
go get <package-name>
```

3. To update the module dependencies, run:

bash

```
go mod tidy
```

Hands-on Examples & Projects

Now, it's time to put theory into practice. We'll walk through some simple Go projects that will help you get comfortable with writing Go code.

Project 1: A Simple Calculator

We will write a basic calculator in Go that can handle simple arithmetic operations like addition, subtraction, multiplication, and division. This will help you practice writing functions and working with user input.

Project 2: Building a To-Do List API

This project will guide you through building a simple REST API using Go's net/http package. You'll learn how to handle HTTP requests, parse JSON data, and structure a basic web server.

Project 3: Web Scraper in Go

We will create a simple web scraper that collects information from a website. This project will introduce you to **HTTP requests**, **HTML parsing**, and **concurrency** with goroutines.

Advanced Techniques & Optimization

As you gain more experience, you will want to optimize your Go applications. In this section, we'll cover performance optimization strategies, advanced concurrency techniques, and ways to manage memory more efficiently.

Troubleshooting and Problem-Solving

While coding, you'll inevitably encounter bugs or errors. This section provides common problems you might face and the best ways to troubleshoot and fix them.

Conclusion & Next Steps

By the end of this chapter, you should feel confident in your ability to start building Go applications. You've learned how to set up your Go environment, understand its core concepts, and write your first Go programs. As you continue your Go journey, remember that the best way to master the language is through practice.

Next steps: Explore more advanced Go topics like web development with Go, cloud applications, and microservices. Dive deeper into the Go community for additional resources and tutorials.

Chapter 2: Mastering Go's Data Types and Variables

Introduction

In the world of programming, **data types** and **variables** serve as the building blocks for any software development project. Whether you're creating a simple program or a large-scale application, understanding how to use variables and data types effectively is essential to writing clean, efficient, and maintainable code. **Go,** as a statically typed language, takes a unique approach to how data types are handled, making it easy for developers to write highly performant and readable code.

In this chapter, we will explore **Go's fundamental data types,** including **integers, strings, floats,** and **booleans,** and dive into more advanced types like **arrays, slices, maps,** and **structs.** These data types are essential for managing data in your Go programs, and mastering them will allow you to create more powerful, efficient applications.

Additionally, we will walk through a hands-on project—a **Contact List App**—that will showcase how to utilize Go's data types and variables in a practical application.

By the end of this chapter, you will not only understand the key data types in Go but also be equipped with the skills to use them in real-world applications. This will form the foundation for building more complex systems in Go, from managing user inputs to processing data.

Core Concepts and Theory

In this section, we will break down the core data types in Go and discuss how to work with them effectively. We'll cover the basic types, how to work with arrays and slices, and introduce more complex data structures like maps and structs. Along the way, we'll use analogies and real-world examples to make these concepts more digestible.

1. Basic Data Types in Go

Go is a statically typed language, meaning that every variable has a specific type that must be declared at compile time. The **basic data types** in Go include integers, floating-point numbers, strings, and booleans.

Integers

An **integer** in Go is a whole number, and it can be either positive or negative. Go supports multiple integer types depending on the size of the number you need to store, such as:

- **int8, int16, int32, int64**: Signed integer types with varying sizes.

- **uint8, uint16, uint32, uint64**: Unsigned integer types with varying sizes (i.e., only positive numbers).

- **int**: The default integer type, whose size is dependent on the platform (32-bit on 32-bit systems, 64-bit on 64-bit systems).

Example:

```go

package main
```

```go
import "fmt"

func main() {
    var a int = 10
    var b int64 = 1000000000
    fmt.Println(a, b)
}
```

Floats

In Go, floating-point numbers are used to represent decimal values. Go supports two types of floating-point numbers:

- **float32**: A 32-bit floating-point number.

- **float64**: A 64-bit floating-point number, which is the default for floating-point operations.

Example:

```go
go

package main

import "fmt"

func main() {
    var pi float64 = 3.14159
    var radius float32 = 2.5
    fmt.Println("Pi:", pi)
    fmt.Println("Radius:", radius)
}
```

Strings

A **string** in Go is a sequence of characters. Strings are immutable, meaning once they are created, they cannot be changed. Go supports string manipulation through various built-in functions and packages like strings.

Example:

```go
go

package main

import "fmt"

func main() {
    var greeting string = "Hello, Go!"
    fmt.Println(greeting)
}
```

Strings in Go are represented as sequences of **bytes**, where each byte represents a character.

Booleans

A **boolean** represents a true or false value. It is commonly used for control flow (e.g., if statements or loops).

Example:

```go
go

package main

import "fmt"

func main() {
    var isActive bool = true
    var isComplete bool = false
    fmt.Println("Active:", isActive)
    fmt.Println("Complete:", isComplete)
}
```

2. Working with Arrays and Slices

Arrays and slices are essential data structures in Go that allow you to work with collections of data.

Arrays

An **array** is a fixed-length sequence of elements of the same type. In Go, the size of an array is part of its type, meaning arrays of different sizes are considered different types.

Example:

```go
package main

import "fmt"

func main() {
    var days [7]string
    days[0] = "Monday"
    days[1] = "Tuesday"
    fmt.Println(days)
}
```

Arrays are generally used for storing a collection of data when the number of elements is known and fixed.

Slices

A **slice** is a more flexible, dynamic version of an array. Unlike arrays, slices can grow or shrink in size during runtime. Slices are a key feature of Go, and they allow you to work with collections more efficiently.

Slices are created using the [] notation and can be created from arrays or as standalone objects using the make() function.

Example:

```go
package main
```

```
import "fmt"

func main() {
    var fruits []string = []string{"Apple",
"Banana", "Cherry"}
    fruits = append(fruits, "Date")
    fmt.Println(fruits)
}
```

- **Slice creation:** Slices can be created using literals (like the example above), or you can create them using the make function with a specified length and capacity.

Example using make():

go

```
fruits := make([]string, 3) // Creates a
slice with a length of 3
fruits[0] = "Apple"
fruits[1] = "Banana"
fruits[2] = "Cherry"
fmt.Println(fruits)
```

3. Understanding Maps and Structs

Maps and structs are more advanced data types that allow you to work with complex, unordered collections of data.

Maps

A **map** is a collection of key-value pairs. The key in a map must be unique, and the values can be of any type. Maps are particularly useful when you need to store data where each value has a unique identifier.

Example:

go

```go
package main

import "fmt"

func main() {
    studentGrades := make(map[string]string)
    studentGrades["John"] = "A"
    studentGrades["Jane"] = "B"
    fmt.Println(studentGrades)
}
```

- **Creating maps**: Maps are created using the make() function, and you can assign and retrieve values using keys.

Structs

A **struct** is a composite data type that groups together variables (fields) under one name. These fields can have different types, making structs ideal for representing more complex data structures such as a contact card, employee record, etc.

Example:

```go
go

package main

import "fmt"

// Define a struct
type Person struct {
    Name  string
    Age   int
    Email string
}
```

```go
func main() {
    // Create a struct instance
    p1 := Person{Name: "Alice", Age: 30,
Email: "alice@example.com"}
    fmt.Println(p1)
}
```

Structs allow you to define custom data types with multiple fields, making them extremely useful for structuring real-world data.

Tools and Setup

Before we dive into hands-on examples and projects, it's important to set up your Go development environment correctly. In this section, we'll go through the necessary tools and setup steps to get you ready for coding with Go.

Step 1: Installing Go

The first step in getting started with Go is installing it on your machine. Go provides installation packages for different operating systems. Follow these steps:

- **Windows**: Download the installer from the Go Downloads page and follow the instructions.

- **macOS**: Use Homebrew or download the .pkg installer.

- **Linux**: Use your package manager or download the tarball from the Go website.

After installation, verify that Go is properly installed by running:

bash

```
go version
```

Step 2: Setting Up the Go Workspace

Go uses a workspace to organize projects. The default workspace includes three directories:

- **src/**: Contains your Go source files.

- **pkg/**: Contains compiled package files.

- **bin/**: Contains executables.

Set up your workspace by creating a go directory and setting the **GOPATH** environment variable:

bash

```
export GOPATH=$HOME/go
export PATH=$PATH:$GOPATH/bin
```

Step 3: Using Go Modules

Go introduced **Go Modules** for managing dependencies in version 1.11. To start using modules, initialize a new module in your project folder:

bash

go mod init myproject

Hands-on Examples & Projects

Now that you've grasped the core concepts and set up your environment, it's time to build something practical.

Building a Contact List App

In this hands-on project, we'll create a **Contact List App** that allows users to store, retrieve, and update contact information using Go's data types.

The app will utilize:

- **Strings** to store names, phone numbers, and email addresses.

- **Arrays/Slices** to store a list of contacts.

- **Maps** for searching contacts by name.

- **Structs** to define the structure of a contact.

Advanced Techniques & Optimization

In this section, we'll dive deeper into advanced techniques for handling large data sets, optimizing memory usage, and working with more complex data structures.

Optimizing Memory Usage with Slices

Slices are flexible but can lead to memory fragmentation if not used efficiently. We'll explore how to optimize slice usage and memory management.

Troubleshooting and Problem-Solving

During development, you'll face common challenges. This section will cover troubleshooting tips, including:

- Handling **index out-of-bounds** errors with arrays and slices.

- Managing **nil values** in structs and maps.

- Fixing **type mismatch** errors.

Conclusion & Next Steps

In this chapter, you've learned about Go's essential data types and how to use them in real-world applications. You now have the foundational skills to build more complex projects. Keep practicing and exploring new ways to leverage Go's data structures in your coding journey.

Next steps: As you move forward, consider diving deeper into Go's **concurrency model** and exploring **error handling** and **file I/O** to enhance your applications.

Happy coding!

Chapter 3: Control Flow and Loops

Introduction

Control flow is a fundamental concept in programming. It refers to the order in which individual statements, instructions, or function calls are executed or evaluated in a program. In Go, as in any programming language, understanding how to manipulate control flow is essential for building complex, efficient, and functional programs. By using control flow mechanisms such as **if-else statements, loops,** and **switch cases,** you can create more interactive and dynamic applications.

In this chapter, we will dive deep into the core control flow concepts in Go, including:

- **Conditionals (if-else statements):** Used to make decisions based on conditions.

- **Loops:** For and range loops to iterate over data.

- **Switch statements:** For multi-way branching.

- **Defer:** For delayed function execution.

These features will help you write more efficient, readable, and flexible code. Throughout this chapter, you will see examples and practical applications, allowing you to grasp these concepts quickly and apply them in your own projects.

One of the most exciting aspects of control flow is its ability to control the flow of execution based on dynamic input and conditions. Whether you're deciding which code to run based on user input or processing a list of items, control flow is crucial for almost every aspect of programming. By the end of this chapter, you will be able to write programs that can make decisions, repeat actions, and handle multiple cases in an organized and efficient manner.

Core Concepts and Theory

Control flow statements are at the heart of most algorithms. Go provides a rich set of control flow constructs, enabling developers to write concise, readable, and efficient code. Let's break down each of the key components you will need to master.

1. Using Conditionals (If-Else Statements)

One of the simplest and most powerful forms of control flow in Go is the **if-else statement**. This allows you to execute a block of code conditionally—only if certain criteria are met.

Basic If-Else Syntax

```go
if condition {
    // Code to run if the condition is true
} else {
    // Code to run if the condition is false
}
```

- **if**: Evaluates the expression or condition.
- **else**: Runs an alternative block of code if the condition is false.

Example: Checking Age

```go
```

```go
package main

import "fmt"

func main() {
    age := 18
    if age >= 18 {
        fmt.Println("You are an adult!")
    } else {
        fmt.Println("You are a minor.")
    }
}
```

In the above code:

- If the variable age is 18 or greater, the program prints "You are an adult!"

- If age is less than 18, it prints "You are a minor."

If-Else If Ladder

You can extend the if-else structure to handle multiple conditions using else if.

```go
go

package main

import "fmt"

func main() {
    score := 85
    if score >= 90 {
        fmt.Println("Grade: A")
    } else if score >= 80 {
        fmt.Println("Grade: B")
    } else {
```

```go
        fmt.Println("Grade: C")
    }
}
```

In this example:

- If the score is 90 or more, it prints "Grade: A".

- If the score is between 80 and 89, it prints "Grade: B".

- Otherwise, it prints "Grade: C".

Shortened If Statement

Go supports a short form of the if statement that allows initialization within the if clause.

```go
go

package main

import "fmt"

func main() {
    if x := 5; x > 0 {
        fmt.Println("Positive number")
    } else {
        fmt.Println("Non-positive number")
    }
}
```

This way, you can initialize x in the if condition and use it within the block.

2. Mastering Loops: For Loops and Range

Loops are an essential part of control flow that allow for the repetitive execution of code. In Go, there is only one looping construct—**the for loop**. It's versatile and can be used for various purposes such as iterating over collections, repeating code a specific number of times, and more.

Basic For Loop

The basic for loop syntax is as follows:

```go
go

for initialization; condition; post {
    // Code to execute
}
```

- **Initialization**: Sets up the loop.

- **Condition**: Tests whether the loop should continue.

- **Post**: Executed after each iteration (typically used to increment a counter).

Example: Counting from 1 to 5

```go
go

package main

import "fmt"

func main() {
    for i := 1; i <= 5; i++ {
        fmt.Println(i)
    }
}
```

In this example:

- The loop initializes i to 1.

- It continues as long as i is less than or equal to 5.

- After each iteration, i is incremented by 1.

While Loop Equivalent

Go does not have a dedicated while loop, but the for loop can be used as one.

```go
package main

import "fmt"

func main() {
    i := 0
    for i < 5 {
        fmt.Println(i)
        i++
    }
}
```

This loop behaves like a while loop, continuing as long as the condition i < 5 is true.

For-Range Loop (Iterating over Collections)

Go's for-range loop allows you to iterate over arrays, slices, strings, maps, and channels. It provides an elegant way to process each element.

```go
package main

import "fmt"

func main() {
    fruits := []string{"Apple", "Banana", "Cherry"}

    for index, value := range fruits {
        fmt.Println(index, value)
```

```
    }
}
```

- **index:** The index of the current element.

- **value:** The value of the current element.

You can omit either the index or the value if it's not needed:

go

```
for _, value := range fruits {
    fmt.Println(value)
}
```

In this case, we are ignoring the index and only printing the values.

3. Switch Statements and Defer

Switch Statement

The switch statement is a cleaner and more readable alternative to multiple if-else statements. It allows for easier comparisons of a variable against multiple values.

Basic Switch Syntax

go

```
switch expression {
case value1:
    // Code if expression == value1
case value2:
    // Code if expression == value2
default:
    // Code if none of the cases match
}
```

Example: Day of the Week

go

```go
package main

import "fmt"

func main() {
    day := 2
    switch day {
    case 1:
        fmt.Println("Monday")
    case 2:
        fmt.Println("Tuesday")
    case 3:
        fmt.Println("Wednesday")
    default:
        fmt.Println("Invalid day")
    }
}
```

In this example:

- The switch checks the value of day and prints the corresponding weekday.

- If the value of day does not match any case, the default case is executed.

Switch with Multiple Conditions

You can also use a switch to check multiple conditions.

```go
go

package main

import "fmt"

func main() {
    number := 7
```

```go
switch {
case number < 0:
    fmt.Println("Negative number")
case number == 0:
    fmt.Println("Zero")
case number > 0:
    fmt.Println("Positive number")
}
}
```

Defer Statement

The defer statement is used to delay the execution of a function until the surrounding function returns. This is useful for handling cleanup operations (e.g., closing a file, unlocking a resource).

```go
go

package main

import "fmt"

func main() {
    defer fmt.Println("This will print last")
    fmt.Println("This will print first")
}
```

In this example:

- The defer statement ensures that the message "This will print last" is printed last, even though it is placed first in the code.

Tools and Setup

Before diving into hands-on examples, let's review the tools and setup required to implement control flow and loops in Go.

Installing Go

Follow the installation process outlined in Chapter 1 to set up your Go environment. You will need the latest stable version of Go installed on your system.

IDE Setup

Using an integrated development environment (IDE) such as **Visual Studio Code (VS Code)** or **GoLand** is highly recommended. These editors offer Go-specific extensions and features like code completion, syntax highlighting, and error checking to improve your development experience.

1. **VS Code Setup:** Install the Go extension from the marketplace.

2. **GoLand Setup:** Download and install from JetBrains for a Go-optimized IDE.

Test the Setup

Once Go is installed, ensure everything is set up correctly by running the following command:

```bash

```

```
go version
```
This will display the current version of Go on your system.

Hands-on Examples & Projects

Building a Number Guessing Game

Now that you have an understanding of control flow and loops, let's apply this knowledge by building a **Number Guessing Game**. This project will utilize **if-else statements**, **for loops**, and **switch statements**.

Step 1: Initialize the Game

```go
package main

import (
    "fmt"
    "math/rand"
    "time"
)

func main() {
    rand.Seed(time.Now().UnixNano()) //
Seed the random number generator
    number := rand.Intn(100) + 1    //
Generate a random number between 1 and 100
    var guess int
    var attempts int

    fmt.Println("Welcome to the Number
Guessing Game!")
    fmt.Println("I have selected a number
between 1 and 100. Try to guess it!")

    // Game loop
    for {
        fmt.Print("Enter your guess: ")
        fmt.Scan(&guess)
```

```
attempts++

if guess < number {
    fmt.Println("Too low!")
} else if guess > number {
    fmt.Println("Too high!")
} else {
    fmt.Printf("Congratulations!
You guessed the number in %d attempts.\n",
attempts)
        break
    }
  }
}
```

- **Game Flow:** This game continuously asks the user for a guess and provides feedback (too high, too low, or correct).

- **Loop:** A for loop keeps the game running until the user guesses the correct number.

Step 2: Adding Difficulty Levels
Enhance the game by adding different difficulty levels that control the number of attempts the user can make. Use a switch statement to handle difficulty choices.

Advanced Techniques & Optimization

Optimizing Control Flow for Large Data Sets
When working with large data sets or complex conditions, optimization becomes crucial. In this section, we explore techniques for improving performance, such as reducing unnecessary iterations and using more efficient algorithms.

Troubleshooting and Problem-Solving

This section will cover common issues that developers encounter while working with control flow in Go, such as:

- **Infinite loops:** Causes and how to fix them.

- **Incorrect conditional logic:** How to debug and test conditions.

- **Performance bottlenecks:** Identifying and optimizing inefficient loops.

Conclusion & Next Steps

This chapter has introduced the key concepts of control flow and loops in Go. You have learned how to use **if-else statements, for loops, switch statements**, and **defer** to control the flow of your programs.

To continue your Go journey, consider learning about more advanced topics like **concurrency, error handling,** and **data structures.** Keep experimenting with control flow structures in your projects to become proficient.

Chapter 4: Functions and Methods in Go

Introduction

In every programming language, **functions** serve as the cornerstone for structuring reusable, modular code. They allow you to break down complex problems into smaller, more manageable tasks, enhancing both the readability and maintainability of your code. In Go, functions play an equally critical role and offer unique features that enhance your ability to write efficient, clean, and concise code.

In this chapter, we'll explore **functions** and **methods** in Go, two closely related concepts that are essential for writing organized programs. You'll learn how to define functions, specify return types, pass parameters, and work with variadic functions. We'll also dive into **methods** on **structs**, an object-oriented concept that allows you to associate behavior with data structures.

Whether you're a beginner, a hobbyist, or an experienced developer, mastering functions and methods will provide you with the tools needed to create more robust and maintainable Go programs.

Why Functions Matter

In any non-trivial software system, you will encounter scenarios where you need to break down a problem into smaller, reusable chunks. Functions allow you to **encapsulate logic** and **abstract details** away from the main execution flow, improving code clarity and reducing redundancy.

Functions are incredibly important because:

- They **encapsulate logic**, allowing code reuse.

- They **simplify** debugging by isolating functionality.

- They improve the **readability** of code, making it easier to understand and modify.

By the end of this chapter, you'll be comfortable with how to use **Go's function system**, including defining functions, working with return values, passing parameters, and even extending them with **methods** on **structs**. Additionally, we'll end the chapter with a hands-on project, where you will create a **simple calculator** to practice using functions in Go.

Core Concepts and Theory

In this section, we will break down Go's function system, explaining key concepts and providing real-world examples to help you understand how to effectively use functions and methods in Go.

1. Defining Functions and Return Types

A **function** is a self-contained block of code that can be called to perform a specific task. In Go, functions are defined using the func keyword. Functions can take zero or more parameters and may return one or more values.

Basic Syntax

Here's the basic syntax for defining a function in Go:

```go

func functionName(parameters) returnType {
    // function body
```

```
}
```

- **func:** This keyword defines a function in Go.

- **functionName:** The name of the function.

- **parameters:** Input parameters, defined with a type.

- **returnType:** The data type of the value the function will return.

Example: Simple Function

Here's a simple example of a function that adds two integers and returns the result:

go

```go
package main

import "fmt"

func add(a int, b int) int {
    return a + b
}

func main() {
    sum := add(5, 3)
    fmt.Println("Sum:", sum)
}
```

In this example:

- **add** is a function that takes two int parameters and returns an int.

- The function is called inside the main function, and the result is printed.

Multiple Return Values

Go allows functions to return multiple values, a feature that is not common in many other programming languages.

```go

package main

import "fmt"

func swap(a, b int) (int, int) {
    return b, a
}

func main() {
    x, y := swap(1, 2)
    fmt.Println("x:", x, "y:", y)
}
```

In this case:

- The swap function returns two integers, and they are unpacked in the main function.

---

2. Function Parameters and Variadic Functions

Passing Parameters

Parameters allow you to pass data into a function. They can be of any data type, and Go is strongly typed, so each parameter must have an explicit type.

Here's an example of a function with multiple parameters:

```go

package main
```

```go
import "fmt"

func multiply(a int, b int) int {
    return a * b
}

func main() {
    result := multiply(4, 6)
    fmt.Println("Multiplication Result:",
result)
}
```

- The function multiply accepts two int parameters and returns their product.

Named Return Values

Go allows you to name the return values of a function. This can help make your code more readable by explicitly indicating what each return value represents.

```go
go

package main

import "fmt"

func divide(a, b int) (result int, err
string) {
    if b == 0 {
        err = "Cannot divide by zero"
        return
    }
    result = a / b
    return
}

func main() {
```

```go
    res, err := divide(10, 0)
    if err != "" {
        fmt.Println(err)
    } else {
        fmt.Println("Result:", res)
    }
}
```

In this example:

- The function divide returns both a result and an error message. The return values are named result and err.

Variadic Functions

A **variadic function** is a function that accepts an arbitrary number of arguments. In Go, this is done by using ... before the parameter type.

Example of a variadic function that sums a series of numbers:

```go
go

package main

import "fmt"

func sum(numbers ...int) int {
    total := 0
    for _, num := range numbers {
        total += num
    }
    return total
}

func main() {
    fmt.Println(sum(1, 2, 3))           //
Outputs 6
```

```go
    fmt.Println(sum(4, 5, 6, 7, 8))      //
Outputs 30
}
```

- The sum function accepts a variable number of int arguments, which are treated as a slice within the function.

- You can pass any number of integers to the function, and it will sum them up.

---

3. Methods on Structs

In Go, methods are similar to functions, but they are associated with a specific type, typically a **struct**. Methods allow you to define behavior that is associated with a data structure, enabling object-oriented design patterns in Go.

Defining Methods

To define a method on a struct, you specify the receiver, which is the type that the method operates on. The receiver is placed before the method name.

```go
go

package main

import "fmt"

type Rectangle struct {
    width   float64
    height float64
}

// Method to calculate the area of the
rectangle
```

```
func (r Rectangle) area() float64 {
    return r.width * r.height
}

func main() {
    rect := Rectangle{width: 5, height: 10}
    fmt.Println("Area:", rect.area())
}
```

In this example:

- Rectangle is a struct with width and height fields.

- The method area() is defined on the Rectangle type and calculates the area.

Pointer Receivers vs Value Receivers

In Go, methods can be defined with either a **value receiver** or a **pointer receiver**. The main difference is that a pointer receiver allows you to modify the underlying value, whereas a value receiver works on a of the value.

Here's the difference between a value receiver and a pointer receiver:

- **Value Receiver**: Works with a of the struct.

- **Pointer Receiver**: Works with the original struct, allowing modification of the original values.

```
go

package main

import "fmt"

type Rectangle struct {
    width  float64
    height float64
```

```
}

// Method with pointer receiver
func (r *Rectangle) scale(factor float64) {
    r.width *= factor
    r.height *= factor
}

func main() {
    rect := Rectangle{width: 5, height: 10}
    rect.scale(2)
    fmt.Println("Scaled Rectangle:", rect)
}
```

In this example:

- The scale method takes a pointer receiver (*Rectangle), so it modifies the original rect object.

Tools and Setup

Before diving into hands-on examples and projects, ensure that your Go development environment is properly set up. This includes installing Go, setting up a workspace, and ensuring you have an appropriate editor.

Step 1: Installing Go

- **Windows:** Download the installer from the Go Downloads page and run the setup wizard.

- **macOS:** You can install Go via Homebrew or download the installer from the Go website.

- **Linux:** Use your package manager, such as apt, or download the Go tarball from the Go website.

Verify the installation by running:

```bash
bash
```

```bash
go version
```

Step 2: Setting Up Your Workspace

Go projects require a workspace where all the code resides. Typically, the workspace consists of three directories:

- src/: Contains the source code.

- pkg/: Contains the compiled package files.

- bin/: Contains executable files.

Set your GOPATH environment variable and configure it to point to the workspace directory:

```bash
bash
```

```bash
export GOPATH=$HOME/go
export PATH=$PATH:$GOPATH/bin
```

Step 3: Choosing an IDE

Although you can use any text editor to write Go code, an integrated development environment (IDE) can boost productivity. Popular IDEs include:

- **GoLand** (IDE by JetBrains, optimized for Go).

- **Visual Studio Code** (VS Code) with the Go extension.

Set up your editor with Go-specific extensions for features like code completion, linting, and debugging.

Hands-on Examples & Projects

Building a Simple Calculator

Let's put everything you've learned so far into practice by building a **Simple Calculator** in Go. This calculator will take user input, perform arithmetic operations, and display the result.

Step 1: Set Up the Basic Structure

We'll start by creating a basic calculator structure, allowing users to choose an operation and input numbers.

```go
package main

import "fmt"

// Function to perform addition
func add(a, b int) int {
    return a + b
}

// Function to perform subtraction
func subtract(a, b int) int {
    return a - b
}

func main() {
    fmt.Println("Welcome to the Simple Calculator")
    var num1, num2 int
    var operation string

    fmt.Print("Enter first number: ")
    fmt.Scan(&num1)
```

```
fmt.Print("Enter second number: ")
fmt.Scan(&num2)
fmt.Print("Enter operation (+, -): ")
fmt.Scan(&operation)

var result int
switch operation {
case "+":
    result = add(num1, num2)
case "-":
    result = subtract(num1, num2)
default:
    fmt.Println("Invalid operation")
    return
}

fmt.Println("Result:", result)
}
```

In this example:

- **Functions:** We've created simple functions for addition and subtraction.

- **Switch Statement:** A switch statement checks the operation chosen by the user.

Step 2: Add More Operations and Error Handling

Enhance the calculator by adding multiplication, division, and error handling for division by zero.

Advanced Techniques & Optimization

Optimizing Functions and Methods

- Using **pointer receivers** instead of value receivers for performance improvement.

- **Tailoring function parameters** to minimize memory usage.

Troubleshooting and Problem-Solving

Common Issues

- **Mismatched function signatures:** How to handle return types and parameters correctly.

- **Scope issues:** Avoiding variable shadowing and understanding variable scope in Go.

Conclusion & Next Steps

By now, you should have a solid understanding of how to define and use functions in Go, as well as how to work with methods on structs. Keep practicing by building new projects, experimenting with different function signatures, and refining your code.

Next Steps: To continue learning, explore more advanced topics such as **interfaces, error handling,** and **Go's concurrency model.** Keep building real-world projects to solidify your knowledge.

Chapter 5: Concurrency in Go: An Introduction

Introduction

In today's fast-paced digital world, building efficient and scalable software is more important than ever. Whether you're building web servers, processing large datasets, or developing real-time systems, **concurrency** is a key concept that enables you to manage multiple tasks simultaneously, making your programs more responsive and efficient.

In Go, concurrency is a first-class citizen, meaning that the language provides built-in mechanisms to handle concurrent tasks in an elegant and easy-to-understand manner. This makes Go an excellent choice for building scalable, high-performance systems that need to handle many tasks at once, such as handling multiple network connections or downloading large files concurrently.

In this chapter, we will introduce you to **concurrency** in Go, explaining its importance and demonstrating how Go's built-in features—**goroutines** and **channels**—allow you to manage concurrent tasks easily. We will also cover **synchronization** techniques using **select statements** and explore how to control the flow of multiple concurrent tasks.

By the end of this chapter, you will have a solid understanding of concurrency in Go and be able to implement efficient and scalable systems that can perform multiple tasks at the same time.

Core Concepts and Theory

Concurrency is one of the standout features of Go. Unlike traditional programming approaches that execute one task at a time, concurrency allows a program to execute multiple tasks simultaneously, improving performance and responsiveness. Let's explore Go's concurrency model and the key concepts involved.

1. What Is Concurrency and Why Is It Important?

Concurrency refers to the ability of a program to execute multiple tasks at the same time. It's important because it allows a program to perform more work in less time, especially on modern hardware with multiple CPU cores.

- **Real-World Analogy**: Imagine you're cooking dinner. If you're only focused on one task at a time, you might first chop vegetables, then cook them, and then set the table. However, if you can handle multiple tasks simultaneously (like chopping while cooking), you can get everything done faster.

In programming, concurrency lets a program handle tasks like:

- **Multiple network requests**: Instead of waiting for one request to complete before starting another, you can handle them concurrently.

- **Real-time systems**: Concurrency is used to respond to multiple events (e.g., user inputs, sensor data) in real-time.

- **Improved performance**: On multi-core processors, concurrent tasks can be executed in parallel, making the program run faster.

Go simplifies concurrency by providing **goroutines** and **channels** as built-in features.

2. Goroutines and Channels Explained

Goroutines

A **goroutine** is a lightweight thread managed by the Go runtime. Goroutines are cheap in terms of memory and are easy to create. You can think of them as lightweight functions that can run concurrently with other goroutines.

Creating a Goroutine

To create a goroutine, simply use the go keyword followed by a function call. This launches the function as a separate concurrent task.

```go

package main

import "fmt"

// A simple function that prints a message
func greet(name string) {
    fmt.Println("Hello,", name)
}

func main() {
    go greet("Alice") // This runs
concurrently with the main function
    go greet("Bob")   // This also runs
concurrently with the main function

    fmt.Println("Main function running...")
}
```

In this example:

- The greet function is called as a goroutine using the go keyword.

- The main function will print "Main function running..." and then exit, but the goroutines will continue running concurrently.

Goroutine Scheduling

Go's runtime schedules goroutines onto available CPU threads. You don't need to worry about managing the threads yourself. The Go runtime takes care of this, allowing you to focus on the tasks at hand.

Channels

Channels are used to communicate between goroutines. They allow one goroutine to send data to another goroutine, and they are a fundamental part of Go's concurrency model. Channels ensure that data is passed safely between goroutines, avoiding race conditions.

A channel is created using the make function:

```go

ch := make(chan int)
```

Sending and Receiving Data through Channels

Once a channel is created, data can be sent into it from one goroutine and received from another.

```go

package main

import "fmt"
```

```
func greet(ch chan string) {
    ch <- "Hello from Goroutine!" // Send a
message into the channel
}

func main() {
    ch := make(chan string)

    go greet(ch)    // Launch a goroutine that
sends data to the channel

    message := <-ch   // Receive the message
from the channel
    fmt.Println(message)
}
```

In this example:

- The greet function sends a message to the channel ch.

- The main function waits for data from the channel using <-ch and then prints it.

Buffered Channels

By default, channels in Go are unbuffered, meaning that the sender must wait for the receiver to read the data. However, you can create **buffered channels** with a specified capacity. This allows the sender to continue without waiting for the receiver.

```go

package main

import "fmt"

func main() {
```

```go
    ch := make(chan string, 2) // Buffered
channel with a capacity of 2
    ch <- "Message 1"
    ch <- "Message 2"

    fmt.Println(<-ch)
    fmt.Println(<-ch)
}
```

In this example:

- The channel ch can hold two messages at once. The
  sender can send both messages into the channel without
  blocking, as long as the channel is not full.

---

3. Synchronization and the Select Statement

In concurrent programming, **synchronization** ensures that
multiple goroutines cooperate correctly and that shared
resources are accessed in a thread-safe manner. Go provides
several ways to synchronize goroutines, and one of the most
powerful tools is the **select** statement.

The Select Statement

The select statement allows a goroutine to wait on multiple
channels. It is similar to a switch statement, but instead of
evaluating expressions, it waits for one of the channels to be
ready for communication.

```go
go

package main

import "fmt"

func main() {
    ch1 := make(chan string)
```

```go
    ch2 := make(chan string)

    go func() { ch1 <- "Channel 1" }()
    go func() { ch2 <- "Channel 2" }()

    select {
    case msg1 := <-ch1:
        fmt.Println("Received from ch1:",
msg1)
    case msg2 := <-ch2:
        fmt.Println("Received from ch2:",
msg2)
    }
}
```

In this example:

- The select statement waits for a message from either ch1 or ch2.

- As soon as one of the channels has data, the corresponding case is executed, and the other channel is ignored.

Timeouts with Select

You can also use select to implement timeouts. For example, you can wait for a channel to receive data for a certain period of time and handle the timeout if it takes too long.

```go

package main

import (
    "fmt"
    "time"
)
```

```
func main() {
    ch := make(chan string)

    go func() {
        time.Sleep(2 * time.Second)
        ch <- "Hello after 2 seconds"
    }()

    select {
    case msg := <-ch:
        fmt.Println(msg)
    case <-time.After(1 * time.Second): //
Timeout after 1 second
        fmt.Println("Timeout: No message
received.")
    }
}
```

In this example:

- If no message is received from the channel within 1
  second, the program prints a timeout message.

Tools and Setup

Before diving into hands-on projects, let's make sure your Go
environment is set up correctly for concurrent programming.

Step 1: Installing Go

Follow the steps from earlier chapters to install Go on your
machine. Ensure that you are using a stable version of Go. You
can check the version of Go by running:

```
bash
```

```
go version
```

Step 2: Choosing an IDE or Text Editor

Go can be written in any text editor, but using an Integrated Development Environment (IDE) or an editor with Go-specific support is highly recommended. Here are some popular options:

- **GoLand**: A specialized IDE from JetBrains designed for Go development.

- **VS Code**: A lightweight editor with the Go extension installed.

- **Sublime Text**: A simple editor with Go support via packages.

These IDEs provide **syntax highlighting, auto-completion**, and **debugging tools** that will make your development process smoother.

Step 3: Setting Up Your Workspace

Go relies on a workspace structure that includes the following directories:

- src/: Contains Go source files.

- pkg/: Contains compiled packages.

- bin/: Contains executable files.

Ensure that your Go workspace is properly set up, and your GOPATH is configured correctly.

Hands-on Examples & Projects

Building a Concurrent File Downloader

Now that you have a solid understanding of Go's concurrency model, let's apply it in a practical project. We will build a **Concurrent File Downloader** that downloads multiple files simultaneously, improving performance and reducing download time.

Step 1: Defining the File Downloader

We'll use Go's goroutines and channels to download multiple files concurrently. For simplicity, we'll simulate file downloads by using time.Sleep.

```go
go

package main

import (
    "fmt"
    "time"
)

func downloadFile(file string, ch chan
string) {
    fmt.Printf("Starting download of
%s...\n", file)
    time.Sleep(2 * time.Second) // Simulate
file download
    ch <- fmt.Sprintf("%s download
complete", file)
}

func main() {
    files := []string{"file1.txt",
"file2.txt", "file3.txt"}
```

```
ch := make(chan string)

for _, file := range files {
    go downloadFile(file, ch) // Start
downloading concurrently
}

for range files {
    fmt.Println(<-ch) // Receive and
print the download status
}
}
```

In this example:

- The downloadFile function simulates downloading a file.

- We start a goroutine for each file in the files list.

- The main function waits for all downloads to complete and prints the results.

Step 2: Handling Multiple Downloads and Timeouts

Now let's add a timeout mechanism to handle scenarios where the download might take too long.

Advanced Techniques & Optimization

Optimizing Concurrency in Go

When working with large numbers of goroutines or high-frequency tasks, optimizing the use of concurrency can lead to significant performance gains. In this section, we'll explore best practices for optimizing concurrency in Go, such as limiting the number of goroutines and minimizing memory usage.

Troubleshooting and Problem-Solving

Common Issues with Goroutines

Some common mistakes with goroutines and channels include:

- **Not properly synchronizing goroutines,** leading to race conditions.

- **Excessive goroutine creation,** leading to high memory usage.

- **Deadlocks** when channels are not closed or handled correctly.

We will provide strategies for debugging and solving these issues in the next section.

Conclusion & Next Steps

In this chapter, we've introduced **concurrency** in Go and explored its key features, including **goroutines, channels,** and the **select statement.** By building a **concurrent file downloader,** you have seen how to apply these concepts in a practical setting.

As you continue exploring Go, consider delving deeper into more advanced topics like **worker pools, error handling** in concurrent systems, and **resource management.**

Keep experimenting with concurrency in Go, as it is a powerful tool for building high-performance, scalable applications.

Chapter 6: Error Handling and Debugging in Go

Introduction

Every programmer knows that errors are an inevitable part of software development. The challenge is not only writing code that works but also handling unexpected situations when something goes wrong. Good error handling can mean the difference between a frustrating debugging experience and a smooth, maintainable codebase.

In Go, error handling is a core part of the language's design. Unlike many other languages that rely on exceptions to manage errors, Go uses a simple but powerful mechanism that involves returning error values. This approach provides greater control over error management and leads to more predictable and maintainable code.

This chapter will introduce you to **error handling** in Go, focusing on how Go's approach to errors differs from other languages, the role of **custom error types**, and how to effectively use **debugging tools** like fmt.Printf to troubleshoot issues in your code. By the end of this chapter, you'll understand how to manage errors efficiently and build robust applications.

In addition to theory, we'll cover practical aspects of error handling and debugging, leading up to a hands-on project where you'll build a **robust file manager** to practice applying these concepts in real-world scenarios.

Core Concepts and Theory

In this section, we'll dive deep into Go's error handling mechanisms, covering key concepts such as custom error types, the error interface, and the use of debugging tools like fmt.Printf.

1. Understanding Go's Approach to Error Handling

In many programming languages, error handling is managed using exceptions. For example, a function may throw an exception if something goes wrong, and you would handle that exception using try-catch blocks. In contrast, Go uses **explicit error handling** where functions return an error value as part of their return signature.

The Error Type

In Go, the error type is a built-in interface that represents an error condition. It's defined as:

```go

type error interface {
    Error() string
}
```

- The Error method on the error interface returns a string that describes the error.

- Any type that implements this method satisfies the error interface, and therefore can be used as an error type.

Error Handling with Multiple Return Values

In Go, many functions return two values: the result of the operation and an error. For example, when working with file I/O or network requests, you will often see functions return the data and an error, as in:

```go
go
```

```go
func someFunction() (result Type, err error)
```

If the function encounters an issue, it returns a non-nil err, and the result is ignored. Otherwise, it returns a valid result and a nil error.

Example: A Function with Error Handling

Consider a simple function that divides two numbers:

```go
go

package main

import (
    "fmt"
    "errors"
)

func divide(a, b int) (int, error) {
    if b == 0 {
        return 0, errors.New("division by
zero is not allowed")
    }
    return a / b, nil
}

func main() {
    result, err := divide(10, 0)
    if err != nil {
        fmt.Println("Error:", err)
    } else {
        fmt.Println("Result:", result)
    }
}
```

In this example:

- The divide function returns an error if the denominator is zero.

- The calling function (main) checks if the error is nil before proceeding with the result.

Why This Approach Works
- **Explicit:** Errors are treated as values, making error handling clear and intentional.

- **Control:** You can choose where and how to handle errors, making it easier to detect and fix issues in your program.

- **Simplicity:** Instead of exceptions that propagate through call stacks, Go's error handling ensures that each function explicitly handles or reports its errors.

2. The Role of Custom Error Types

While Go's built-in error type is simple and effective, there are times when you need to create your own custom error types to convey more information about an error. Go allows you to define custom error types by creating a new type that implements the Error() method.

Creating a Custom Error Type

To define a custom error, you create a struct type that contains relevant data (like an error message or error code), and then implement the Error() method on that struct.

```go
go

package main

import (
    "fmt"
```

```go
)

type DivisionError struct {
    Divisor int
    Message string
}

func (e *DivisionError) Error() string {
    return fmt.Sprintf("Error: %s (divisor:
%d)", e.Message, e.Divisor)
}

func divide(a, b int) (int, error) {
    if b == 0 {
        return 0, &DivisionError{Divisor: b,
Message: "division by zero"}
    }
    return a / b, nil
}

func main() {
    result, err := divide(10, 0)
    if err != nil {
        fmt.Println("Error:", err)
    } else {
        fmt.Println("Result:", result)
    }
}
```

In this example:

- We define a DivisionError struct with two fields: Divisor and Message.

- The Error() method formats the custom error message.

- The divide function returns this custom error when division by zero is attempted.

Benefits of Custom Error Types

- **Additional Context**: Custom errors allow you to embed additional information (like an error code or parameters related to the error) that can be useful for troubleshooting.

- **Error Hierarchy**: Custom errors can help you define a clear hierarchy of errors, making it easier to handle specific error types differently.

---

3. Debugging Go Code with Printf and Other Tools

When it comes to debugging, Go provides several tools to help you track down and fix issues. The most basic form of debugging involves using fmt.Printf to print values at different points in the program.

Using fmt.Printf for Debugging

fmt.Printf is useful for inspecting variables and understanding the flow of execution. Here's an example:

```go
package main

import "fmt"

func main() {
    a := 5
    b := 0

    fmt.Printf("a = %d, b = %d\n", a, b)
    if b == 0 {
```

```
        fmt.Println("Error: division by
zero")
    } else {
        fmt.Println("Result:", a/b)
    }
}
```

- This will print the values of a and b before the division attempt, helping you understand the state of the program at that point.

The Debugging Tools in Go

For more advanced debugging, Go offers several other tools and techniques:

- **Delve:** Delve is a powerful debugger for Go programs. It allows you to set breakpoints, step through code, inspect variables, and more.

- **Go's pprof Package:** The pprof package can be used for profiling your Go programs to detect performance bottlenecks and memory leaks.

Setting Up Delve

To install Delve, run the following command:

```bash

go get github.com/go-delve/delve/cmd/dlv
```

Once installed, you can start debugging a Go program with Delve:

```bash

dlv debug main.go
```

Delve provides a REPL where you can set breakpoints, step through your code, and inspect values. This is especially useful for more complex programs where printing values with fmt.Printf isn't enough.

Tools and Setup

Before diving into practical examples and projects, let's ensure you have the right tools and environment set up for effective error handling and debugging.

Step 1: Installing Go

Ensure that you have the latest version of Go installed on your machine. If you haven't already, follow these steps:

- **Windows**: Download the Go installer from the Go Downloads page and follow the setup wizard.

- **macOS**: You can install Go via Homebrew or download the .pkg installer.

- **Linux**: Use your package manager (e.g., apt, yum) or download the Go tarball.

To verify the installation, run:

```bash

go version
```

Step 2: Choosing an IDE

While you can use any text editor, Go-specific IDEs like **GoLand** or editors like **VS Code** (with the Go extension) will make development easier. These tools offer:

- **Syntax highlighting**
- **Code completion**

- Integrated debugging

Step 3: Installing Debugging Tools

For advanced debugging, you may want to install **Delve**. Run the following command to install it:

```bash
go get github.com/go-delve/delve/cmd/dlv
```

For profiling, you can also install Go's built-in **pprof** package for performance analysis.

Hands-on Examples & Projects

Building a Robust File Manager

In this hands-on section, we will build a simple **file manager** that supports common file operations like reading, writing, and deleting files. The goal is to handle errors gracefully, use custom error types, and implement robust error handling for different scenarios.

Step 1: Defining the File Manager

```go
package main

import (
    "fmt"
    "io/ioutil"
    "os"
)

// Custom error type for file operations
type FileError struct {
```

```
    Op  string
    Err error
}

func (e *FileError) Error() string {
    return fmt.Sprintf("File operation %s
failed: %v", e.Op, e.Err)
}

// Function to read a file
func readFile(filename string) (string,
error) {
    data, err := ioutil.ReadFile(filename)
    if err != nil {
        return "", &FileError{Op: "read",
Err: err}
    }
    return string(data), nil
}

// Function to write data to a file
func writeFile(filename, data string) error
{
    err := ioutil.WriteFile(filename,
[]byte(data), 0644)
    if err != nil {
        return &FileError{Op: "write", Err:
err}
    }
    return nil
}

func main() {
    // Example usage of the file manager
    filename := "example.txt"

    // Write to file
```

```go
    if err := writeFile(filename, "Hello,
Go!"); err != nil {
        fmt.Println(err)
        return
    }

    // Read from file
    content, err := readFile(filename)
    if err != nil {
        fmt.Println(err)
        return
    }

    fmt.Println("File content:", content)
}
```

In this example:

- We define a **custom error type** (FileError) to handle file operation errors.

- We implement two functions: readFile and writeFile, each returning an error when an operation fails.

- The program prints the error if any operation fails.

Step 2: Adding More Robust Error Handling

Expand this file manager to handle more complex cases such as checking for file existence and handling different types of file errors.

Advanced Techniques & Optimization

Optimizing Error Handling for Performance

While Go's error handling approach is simple, it can become cumbersome when handling large numbers of errors or highly concurrent applications. In this section, we'll explore strategies for **optimizing error handling** to avoid performance bottlenecks and maintain clean code.

Troubleshooting and Problem-Solving

Common Mistakes in Error Handling

- **Ignoring errors**: A common mistake in Go is ignoring errors by assigning them to a blank identifier (_). This can lead to unnoticed failures.

- **Unnecessary error wrapping**: While Go encourages explicit error handling, excessive wrapping of errors can make debugging harder. We'll explore how to balance error propagation with clarity.

- **Not handling nil errors properly**: Sometimes, the err variable may be nil when expected, leading to faulty logic in the program.

We'll provide strategies for debugging these issues and help you avoid these pitfalls.

Conclusion & Next Steps

In this chapter, we've covered **error handling** and **debugging** in Go, two essential skills for writing robust and maintainable code. You've learned:

- How Go handles errors using the error type and multiple return values.

- How to create **custom error types** for more granular error information.

- How to use **debugging tools** like fmt.Printf and **Delve** to troubleshoot issues.

For the next steps:

- Continue practicing error handling in different contexts.

- Experiment with Go's debugging tools to improve your workflow.

- Explore **advanced error handling** techniques like using errors.Is and errors.As for better error propagation.

Keep building, experimenting, and refining your Go programming skills!

Chapter 7: Structuring and Organizing Go Projects

Introduction

One of the key elements of writing clean, maintainable software is knowing how to structure and organize your project. Whether you're working on a small script or a large-scale application, how you organize your code can significantly impact its readability, scalability, and ease of maintenance. Go, like any other programming language, provides a variety of ways to structure projects, and adopting the right structure from the start can make your development process much smoother.

In this chapter, we will explore how to structure and organize Go projects in a way that promotes **modularity, reusability**, and **scalability**. We'll also look at best practices for organizing your Go code into **packages** and **directories**, ensuring that your project remains maintainable and easy to navigate as it grows.

The chapter is aimed at beginners, professionals, and hobbyists alike, providing an in-depth understanding of Go project organization principles. We'll cover:

- **Project structure:** How to organize your files and directories.

- **Package organization:** Understanding how to use packages to create modular code.

- **Best practices** for code modularity and maintaining clean code.

- A **hands-on exercise** where you'll apply these principles by building a **To-Do List API** in Go, which will reinforce the concepts and techniques discussed.

By the end of this chapter, you will be able to structure Go projects efficiently, making them easier to maintain and scale.

Core Concepts and Theory

In Go, structuring and organizing your code is just as important as writing it. Proper organization allows you to build scalable and maintainable applications that will be easy to extend, refactor, and debug. Let's explore the core concepts involved in structuring Go projects, including package organization, directory structure, and best practices for modularity.

1. How to Structure Your Go Projects

When starting a new Go project, the way you organize your files and directories can make a huge difference in the long term. Go projects typically follow a standard layout to ensure consistency and clarity. Below is a common structure that you can use as a guideline for your Go applications.

Basic Directory Layout

A typical Go project might look like this:

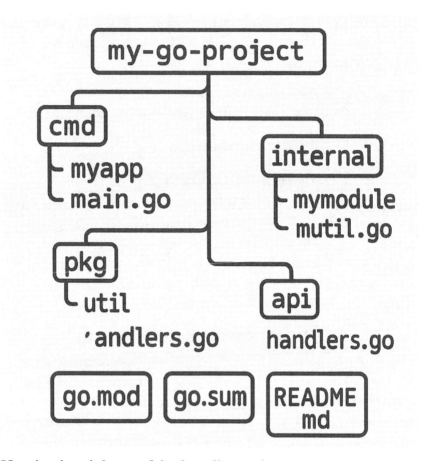

Here's a breakdown of the key directories:

- **cmd/**: This directory contains the application's entry point. If you have multiple applications (e.g., a CLI tool and a web server), they would each have their own subdirectory under cmd/. For example, in this case, myapp contains main.go, the entry point for the application.

- **internal/**: This directory is for packages that are meant to be private to the project. Any code here is **not** accessible outside the module, which is a Go-specific convention that helps prevent accidental misuse of internal components.

- **pkg/**: This directory contains code that is meant to be shared or reused across the project. It might include utility functions, libraries, or other code that could be useful in different parts of the project.

- **api/**: This directory holds code related to external communication, such as API handlers, server logic, or protocols.

- **go.mod and go.sum**: These files are used for managing dependencies in your Go project, similar to package managers in other languages like npm or pip.

Why This Layout Works
The layout encourages modularity by:

- Isolating private (internal) code from public (shared) code.

- Encouraging a clear separation between application-specific logic (cmd/) and reusable modules (pkg/).

- Making it easier to navigate and understand the structure of the project as it grows.

2. Understanding Package Organization

Go's package system allows you to logically group related functions and types together, making your code easier to manage and test. A **package** in Go is simply a collection of related Go files. Go packages are designed to be simple, focused, and well-organized.

Package Organization Principles

- **Single Responsibility**: Each package should have one responsibility, and it should encapsulate functionality related to that responsibility. For example, if you're building a web application, you might have separate packages for database access, API routes, and authentication.

- **Naming Conventions**: Package names should be concise and reflect the purpose of the package. For example, a package for working with user authentication might be called auth, and a package for database handling could be named db.

- **Exported vs Unexported Names**: In Go, names of variables, functions, and types that begin with an uppercase letter are **exported** and can be accessed outside the package. Names that begin with a lowercase letter are **unexported** and can only be used within the package.

Example of a Simple Package:

Let's create a basic utility package called mathutils to perform simple arithmetic operations.

```go
// mathutils/mathutils.go
package mathutils

// Add returns the sum of two integers
func Add(a, b int) int {
    return a + b
}
```

```go
// Subtract returns the difference between
two integers
func Subtract(a, b int) int {
    return a - b
}
go

// main.go
package main

import (
    "fmt"
    "my-go-project/pkg/mathutils"
)

func main() {
    fmt.Println(mathutils.Add(5, 3))    // Output: 8
    fmt.Println(mathutils.Subtract(5, 3)) // Output: 2
}
```

In this example:

- We define the mathutils package with two functions: Add and Subtract.

- The main function in the cmd/myapp directory imports and uses the functions from mathutils.

3. Best Practices for Code Modularity

Modular code is essential for building maintainable applications. Code modularity makes it easier to test individual parts, debug, and extend functionality without affecting other areas of the project. Let's look at some best practices for modularizing your Go code.

Separation of Concerns

Each package should be focused on a specific concern or responsibility. For example:

- A db package handles all database-related operations.

- An auth package manages user authentication and authorization.

- A handler package is responsible for handling HTTP requests.

This separation helps with **code reusability** and **maintainability**. If a bug arises in one part of the application, it is easier to locate and fix because the code is organized by concern.

Small, Focused Functions

Each function should have a single responsibility and should do one thing well. Functions that are too large or try to do too many things become difficult to test and maintain. For example:

```go
// Good
func AuthenticateUser(username, password
string) (User, error) {
    // Authentication logic here
}

// Bad
func AuthenticateAndAuthorizeUser(username,
password string) (User, error) {
    // Authentication and authorization
logic here
    // Too many responsibilities for a
single function
```

```
}
```

Encapsulation

Encapsulation ensures that internal logic is hidden from the outside world, exposing only the necessary parts. This is one of the principles of **information hiding** and **abstraction** in object-oriented design. In Go, you achieve encapsulation using **unexported types** and **methods**.

```go
// db/db.go
package db

type Connection struct {
    // unexported fields
}

func (c *Connection) Connect() {
    // connection logic
}

func NewConnection() *Connection {
    return &Connection{}
}
```

In this example:

- The Connection struct is unexported, and its fields are inaccessible outside the package.

- Only the Connect method and NewConnection constructor are exposed.

Tools and Setup

Before we jump into the practical examples, let's make sure your development environment is properly set up for structuring Go projects. We'll cover the tools and platforms needed for this chapter.

Step 1: Installing Go

Ensure you have Go installed and correctly configured on your system. Refer to the earlier chapters for installation instructions. To verify that Go is installed properly, run the following command in your terminal:

```
bash
```

```
go version
```
This will display the Go version you have installed.

Step 2: Setting Up Your Go Workspace

Go relies on a workspace to organize your code. You can configure your workspace by setting up the GOPATH and GOBIN environment variables. Here's how you can do that:

```
bash
```

```
export GOPATH=$HOME/go
export GOBIN=$GOPATH/bin
export PATH=$PATH:$GOBIN
```

Step 3: Choosing an Editor/IDE

Using an integrated development environment (IDE) can make Go development easier. Some popular options include:

- **GoLand:** A powerful IDE specifically designed for Go development.

- **VS Code:** A lightweight code editor with Go extensions.

- **Sublime Text**: A fast and minimal text editor that supports Go through plugins.

Ensure your chosen IDE has Go support enabled, including syntax highlighting, auto-completion, and debugging tools.

Hands-on Examples & Projects

Building a To-Do List API

Now that you understand how to structure Go projects, it's time to put that knowledge into practice. We'll build a simple **To-Do List API**. This API will allow users to create, retrieve, and delete to-do items.

Step 1: Define the Project Structure

Let's start by defining the project structure:

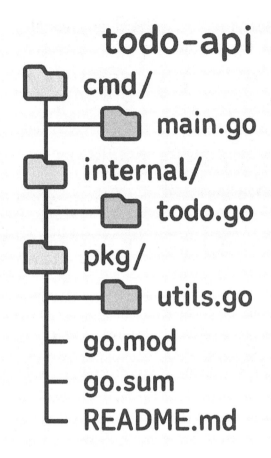

- **cmd/api/**: This will contain the entry point (main.go) of our API server.

- **internal/todo/**: Contains the core logic for managing to-do items.

- **pkg/utils/**: Contains utility functions (e.g., for validation or formatting).

Step 2: Create the To-Do Package
First, we create the todo package to handle our to-do items.

```go

// internal/todo/todo.go
package todo

import "fmt"

// Todo represents a single to-do item
type Todo struct {
    ID   int
    Task string
}

// TodoList is a collection of todos
var TodoList = []Todo{}

// Create adds a new to-do to the list
func Create(task string) Todo {
    id := len(TodoList) + 1
    newTodo := Todo{ID: id, Task: task}
    TodoList = append(TodoList, newTodo)
    return newTodo
}

// GetAll returns all to-do items
func GetAll() []Todo {
    return TodoList
}
```

Step 3: Implement the API Handlers

Next, we define the API handlers in cmd/api/main.go.

```go

// cmd/api/main.go
package main
```

```go
import (
    "fmt"
    "net/http"
    "my-go-project/internal/todo"
    "encoding/json"
)

func createTodoHandler(w
http.ResponseWriter, r *http.Request) {
    task := r.URL.Query().Get("task")
    newTodo := todo.Create(task)
    w.WriteHeader(http.StatusCreated)
    json.NewEncoder(w).Encode(newTodo)
}

func getTodosHandler(w http.ResponseWriter,
r *http.Request) {
    todos := todo.GetAll()
    w.WriteHeader(http.StatusOK)
    json.NewEncoder(w).Encode(todos)
}

func main() {
    http.HandleFunc("/todos",
getTodosHandler)
    http.HandleFunc("/create",
createTodoHandler)

    fmt.Println("Starting server on :8080")
    http.ListenAndServe(":8080", nil)
}
```

In this example:

- The /todos route fetches all to-dos.

- The /create route allows users to add a new to-do item.

Step 4: Run the Application

1. Run go run cmd/api/main.go to start the server.

2. Use curl or Postman to test the API.

Advanced Techniques & Optimization

Optimizing Code Modularity and Performance

- **Separation of concerns**: Continue separating different application layers into different packages (e.g., separating API handlers from database logic).

- **Caching**: Implement caching mechanisms for frequently accessed data to improve performance.

- **Database Integration**: Swap in a database package like gorm or sqlx for persistent data storage.

Troubleshooting and Problem-Solving

Common Issues with Project Structure

- **Circular dependencies**: Learn how to avoid circular dependencies between packages.

- **Improper package organization**: How to refactor and reorganize packages for better maintainability.

Conclusion & Next Steps

In this chapter, you learned how to structure and organize Go projects effectively. You explored how to:

- Structure your Go project using directories like cmd, pkg, and internal.

- Modularize your code by creating reusable packages.

- Implement best practices for scalability and maintainability.

Next, continue experimenting with larger projects and practice organizing code for more complex applications. Explore advanced topics like **dependency injection, middleware**, and **unit testing** to further refine your skills.

Keep coding and building!

Chapter 8: Working with External Libraries and APIs

Introduction

In modern software development, it's rare that you'll write every piece of functionality from scratch. Rather, most of the time, you'll rely on **external libraries** and **APIs** (Application Programming Interfaces) to speed up development and access services that are outside of your own codebase. Go, as a powerful programming language, has robust support for integrating with these external resources.

This chapter will dive into how to effectively work with **third-party libraries** and **APIs** in Go, two essential aspects of building real-world applications. We'll begin by discussing how to install and use external libraries to enhance your Go applications. After that, we will cover **HTTP requests** and **JSON handling**, which are fundamental for interacting with external services and APIs.

In the second half of this chapter, we'll build a **weather application** that consumes a weather API to retrieve data and display it to the user. This hands-on exercise will demonstrate the concepts discussed, helping you learn how to integrate external libraries and APIs into your Go projects.

By the end of this chapter, you'll have a solid understanding of how to use third-party libraries and APIs in Go and how to structure your Go code to interact with these external resources efficiently.

Core Concepts and Theory

This section will provide in-depth coverage of essential concepts required to interact with third-party libraries and APIs in Go. We will cover topics like installing and using external libraries, making HTTP requests, handling JSON data, and best practices when working with APIs in Go.

1. Installing and Using Third-Party Libraries

Go has an excellent package management system that allows you to install and use third-party libraries easily. Go modules, introduced in Go 1.11, allow for easy management of dependencies and versioning, making it simpler to work with external libraries.

Using Go Modules

Go uses modules to manage dependencies. A Go module is essentially a collection of Go packages, with each package in the module specifying its version. To begin using external libraries in Go, you must first initialize a Go module.

To initialize a Go module in your project, run the following command:

```bash
```

```
go mod init <module-name>
```
This will create a go.mod file that keeps track of all the dependencies for your project.

Installing External Libraries

To install an external library, you can use the go get command followed by the package URL. For example, to install the gorilla/mux package, which is a popular HTTP router for Go, run:

bash

```
go get github.com/gorilla/mux
```

Once the library is installed, it will be added to your go.mod file, and you can import and use it in your project.

Example of Using an External Library:

Let's see how you would use the gorilla/mux router in a simple web server.

go

```
package main

import (
    "fmt"
    "github.com/gorilla/mux"
    "net/http"
)

func HelloWorld(w http.ResponseWriter, r
*http.Request) {
    fmt.Fprintf(w, "Hello, world!")
}

func main() {
    r := mux.NewRouter()
    r.HandleFunc("/", HelloWorld)
    http.Handle("/", r)
    http.ListenAndServe(":8080", nil)
}
```

In this example:

- We installed the gorilla/mux package using go get.

- We used it to create a new HTTP router (r), which is then used to handle requests to the root URL ("/").

Updating Dependencies

You can update the dependencies in your project by running:

```bash
go get -u <library-name>
```

This will download the latest version of the specified library and update your go.mod file accordingly.

2. Making HTTP Requests and Handling JSON

HTTP requests are the primary way to interact with external APIs, and JSON is the most common data format used for exchanging information between a client and a server. Go provides a powerful standard library for making HTTP requests and handling JSON data.

Making HTTP Requests

In Go, you can use the net/http package to make HTTP requests. Here's an example of how to send a simple GET request to an API:

```go
package main

import (
    "fmt"
    "io/ioutil"
    "net/http"
)

func main() {
    response, err :=
http.Get("https://api.openweathermap.org/dat
a/2.5/weather?q=London&appid=your_api_key")
    if err != nil {
```

```
        fmt.Println("Error making GET
request:", err)
        return
    }
    defer response.Body.Close()

    body, err :=
ioutil.ReadAll(response.Body)
    if err != nil {
        fmt.Println("Error reading response
body:", err)
        return
    }

    fmt.Println("Response Body:",
string(body))
}
```

In this example:

- We use http.Get to send a GET request to a weather API.

- We check for errors during the request and response reading process.

- The response body is read into a byte slice using ioutil.ReadAll.

Handling JSON Data

JSON is a popular data format, and Go makes it simple to work with using the encoding/json package. To decode JSON data into Go structures, we need to define the appropriate structs and use json.Unmarshal.

Here's how you can parse JSON data from an API response:

go

```go
package main

import (
    "encoding/json"
    "fmt"
    "io/ioutil"
    "net/http"
)

type Weather struct {
    Name string `json:"name"`
    Main struct {
        Temp float64 `json:"temp"`
    } `json:"main"`
}

func main() {
    response, err :=
http.Get("https://api.openweathermap.org/dat
a/2.5/weather?q=London&appid=your_api_key")
    if err != nil {
        fmt.Println("Error making GET
request:", err)
        return
    }
    defer response.Body.Close()

    body, err :=
ioutil.ReadAll(response.Body)
    if err != nil {
        fmt.Println("Error reading response
body:", err)
        return
    }

    var weather Weather
```

```go
    err = json.Unmarshal(body, &weather)
    if err != nil {
        fmt.Println("Error unmarshalling
JSON:", err)
        return
    }

    fmt.Printf("City: %s, Temperature:
%.2f°C\n", weather.Name, weather.Main.Temp-
273.15)
}
```

In this example:

- We define a Weather struct that corresponds to the structure of the JSON data returned by the weather API.

- We use json.Unmarshal to decode the JSON data into the struct.

- The temperature is converted from Kelvin to Celsius.

POST Requests and Sending JSON

To send JSON data to an API, you can use http.NewRequest or http.Post along with the encoding/json package to encode your data.

```go
package main

import (
    "bytes"
    "encoding/json"
    "fmt"
    "net/http"
)
```

```go
type PostData struct {
    Name  string `json:"name"`
    Email string `json:"email"`
}

func main() {
    data := PostData{Name: "John Doe",
Email: "john.doe@example.com"}
    jsonData, err := json.Marshal(data)
    if err != nil {
        fmt.Println("Error marshalling
data:", err)
        return
    }

    response, err :=
http.Post("https://example.com/api",
"application/json",
bytes.NewBuffer(jsonData))
    if err != nil {
        fmt.Println("Error making POST
request:", err)
        return
    }
    defer response.Body.Close()

    fmt.Println("Response Status:",
response.Status)
}
```

In this example:

- We use json.Marshal to convert the Go struct into JSON format.

- We then send the JSON data in a POST request using http.Post.

3. Best Practices for Working with APIs in Go

When working with external APIs in Go, there are several best practices you should follow to ensure that your application remains robust, secure, and maintainable.

1. Handle Errors Gracefully

Always check for errors when making HTTP requests and decoding responses. Network issues, timeouts, and incorrect responses are common when dealing with external APIs, so it's important to handle errors correctly.

2. Limit External Requests

APIs often have rate limits, which restrict the number of requests you can make in a given period. Make sure to respect these limits to avoid being blocked from the API. You can also implement caching strategies to reduce the number of API calls.

3. Secure API Keys

API keys are sensitive and should never be hardcoded in your code. Instead, store them in environment variables or configuration files that are not checked into version control.

4. Use Go Routines for Concurrent Requests

Go makes it easy to send multiple requests concurrently using **goroutines**. This can be particularly useful if you need to retrieve data from multiple APIs or make several requests in parallel.

Tools and Setup

Before we dive into the hands-on examples, let's ensure that your development environment is set up for working with external libraries and APIs.

Step 1: Installing Go

Ensure you have Go installed by running the following:

```bash
bash
```

```bash
go version
```

If you don't have Go installed, follow the installation guide for your operating system from the official Go website.

Step 2: Setting Up Dependencies

In your Go project, initialize the Go module to manage dependencies:

```bash
bash
```

```bash
go mod init <module-name>
```

To install a third-party library, use go get:

```bash
bash
```

```bash
go get github.com/gorilla/mux
```

For JSON handling, you don't need to install any external packages since Go's encoding/json package is included by default.

Hands-on Examples & Projects

Building a Weather App with External API

Now that we understand the concepts, it's time to build a simple **Weather App** that fetches data from the OpenWeatherMap API.

Step 1: Set Up the Weather API

1. Create a free account at OpenWeatherMap.

2. Get your **API key** from the dashboard.

Step 2: Fetch Weather Data

We will use the http package to send a GET request to OpenWeatherMap's API and handle the JSON response.

```go
package main

import (
    "encoding/json"
    "fmt"
    "io/ioutil"
    "net/http"
)

type Weather struct {
    Name string `json:"name"`
    Main struct {
        Temp float64 `json:"temp"`
    } `json:"main"`
}

func main() {
```

```go
    response, err :=
http.Get("https://api.openweathermap.org/dat
a/2.5/weather?q=London&appid=your_api_key")
    if err != nil {
        fmt.Println("Error making GET
request:", err)
        return
    }
    defer response.Body.Close()

    body, err :=
ioutil.ReadAll(response.Body)
    if err != nil {
        fmt.Println("Error reading response
body:", err)
        return
    }

    var weather Weather
    err = json.Unmarshal(body, &weather)
    if err != nil {
        fmt.Println("Error unmarshalling
JSON:", err)
        return
    }

    fmt.Printf("City: %s, Temperature:
%.2f°C\n", weather.Name, weather.Main.Temp-
273.15)
}
```

Step 3: Run the Application

Run the Go file and verify that the weather details for your city are displayed.

Advanced Techniques & Optimization

Optimizing API Requests for Scalability

- **Rate Limiting**: Implement a rate limiter to ensure that your API doesn't exceed the limits set by the external API.

- **Concurrency**: Use Go's goroutines to handle multiple API requests concurrently, improving performance for applications that need to query multiple APIs.

Troubleshooting and Problem-Solving

Common Issues When Working with APIs

- **Invalid API Key**: Ensure that your API key is correct and stored securely.

- **JSON Decoding Errors**: Always check for proper struct mappings when decoding JSON responses.

- **Network Errors**: Handle network issues gracefully by retrying failed requests and informing the user about connectivity problems.

Conclusion & Next Steps

In this chapter, you've learned how to:

- Install and use third-party libraries in Go.

- Make HTTP requests and handle JSON data.

- Apply best practices for working with external APIs.

You've also built a **weather app** using an external API, reinforcing these concepts in a practical project. As you continue to work with APIs in Go, explore more advanced topics like **authentication** with APIs, **pagination** of results, and **error handling** for external APIs.

Keep building and experimenting with Go to enhance your skills in integrating third-party libraries and APIs into your projects.

Chapter 9: Writing Unit Tests in Go

Introduction

Testing is an integral part of modern software development, and Go is no exception. Whether you're writing a small script or a large-scale application, ensuring that your code behaves as expected is essential for delivering high-quality software. This is where **unit testing** comes in.

Unit tests are automated tests that validate individual pieces of code (usually functions) to ensure that they work correctly. They are fundamental for **debugging, refactoring,** and ensuring that your code is **maintainable** and **robust** over time. Go provides a built-in package called testing that makes writing unit tests straightforward and effective.

In this chapter, we will dive into:

- The **importance of testing** in Go development and why it should be a priority for every developer.

- How to **write unit tests** using Go's testing package.

- Techniques for **mocking** external dependencies to make unit tests isolated and reliable.

- How to measure **test coverage** and improve the overall quality of your codebase.

We will also walk through a hands-on exercise where we will build a **user authentication module** and write tests for it, helping you understand how to apply these concepts to real-world projects.

By the end of this chapter, you will have a solid understanding of how to write unit tests in Go, integrate them into your development workflow, and ensure that your applications are reliable and bug-free.

Core Concepts and Theory

Unit testing in Go is built around the testing package, but before diving into the syntax, let's first understand why testing is crucial and how to structure tests in Go.

1. Why Testing is Crucial in Go Development

Testing ensures that your code performs as expected, even when you make changes or add new features. In Go, unit testing is a natural extension of the language's design, allowing you to ensure that your code remains clean, maintainable, and free of bugs.

Key Benefits of Unit Testing in Go:

- **Early bug detection:** Unit tests help identify bugs at an early stage, making it easier and cheaper to fix issues.

- **Refactoring with confidence:** With a solid suite of tests, you can confidently refactor your code, knowing that any breakages will be caught by tests.

- **Increased code quality:** Writing unit tests forces you to think more about the design and structure of your code, leading to better software.

- **Documentation:** Unit tests act as **living documentation,** providing clear examples of how your functions should behave.

Why Go?

Go's simplicity and performance-oriented design make it a great choice for writing reliable and efficient unit tests. It includes the testing package, which is easy to use and integrates well with Go's build and test tools.

2. How to Write Unit Tests with the Testing Package

The Go testing package is designed for writing and running unit tests. Writing unit tests involves creating functions that begin with Test and then using assertions to check if the code behaves as expected.

Basic Test Function Structure

A basic test function in Go follows this pattern:

```go
package mypackage

import "testing"

// Function to test
func Add(a, b int) int {
    return a + b
}

// Test function
func TestAdd(t *testing.T) {
    result := Add(2, 3)
    expected := 5
    if result != expected {
```

```
      t.Errorf("Add(2, 3) = %d; expected
%d", result, expected)
    }
}
```

- **Test function signature**: The function should be named TestX where X is the name of the function being tested.

- **Testing parameter**: The function takes a pointer to testing.T to report errors and failures.

- **Assertions**: Inside the test function, use t.Errorf() to report failures when the result does not match the expected value.

Running Tests

To run the tests, you can use the following command:

```bash
```

```
go test
```

This command will automatically find all the test functions (those starting with Test) and run them.

Example of a Simple Test

Let's write a test for a simple Multiply function:

```go
```

```
// multiply.go
package mypackage

// Multiply multiplies two integers
func Multiply(a, b int) int {
    return a * b
}
```

Now, let's write a test for the Multiply function:

```go
// multiply_test.go
package mypackage

import "testing"

func TestMultiply(t *testing.T) {
    result := Multiply(2, 3)
    expected := 6
    if result != expected {
        t.Errorf("Multiply(2, 3) = %d;
expected %d", result, expected)
    }
}
```

When you run go test, it will automatically check if Multiply(2, 3) returns 6. If it does not, the test will fail and print the error message.

3. Mocking in Go

Often, unit tests need to interact with external systems, like databases or APIs. This can make tests slow, unreliable, and difficult to isolate. To solve this, you can use **mocking** to simulate these external systems.

What is Mocking?

Mocking is the process of replacing a real object or function with a simulated one that behaves in a controlled way. This is useful for testing units in isolation without depending on external systems.

Go doesn't have built-in mocking tools, but several libraries can help, including:

- **GoMock**: A popular mocking framework for Go.

- **Testify:** A toolkit that provides assertion functions and mock objects.

Example of Mocking with Testify

Let's mock a database interaction in a function that retrieves user data.

go

```
package mypackage

import "github.com/stretchr/testify/mock"

// UserService is a service that retrieves
user data from the database
type UserService struct {
    DB Database
}

type Database interface {
    GetUser(id int) (User, error)
}

type User struct {
    ID    int
    Name string
}

func (s *UserService) GetUser(id int) (User,
error) {
    return s.DB.GetUser(id)
}
```

Now, let's mock the Database interface and test UserService:

go

```
package mypackage
```

```go
import (
    "testing"
    "github.com/stretchr/testify/mock"
    "github.com/stretchr/testify/assert"
)

// MockDatabase is a mock of the Database
interface
type MockDatabase struct {
    mock.Mock
}

func (m *MockDatabase) GetUser(id int)
(User, error) {
    args := m.Called(id)
    return args.Get(0).(User), args.Error(1)
}

func TestGetUser(t *testing.T) {
    mockDB := new(MockDatabase)
    mockDB.On("GetUser", 1).Return(User{ID:
1, Name: "John Doe"}, nil)

    userService := &UserService{DB: mockDB}

    user, err := userService.GetUser(1)

    assert.NoError(t, err)
    assert.Equal(t, "John Doe", user.Name)
    mockDB.AssertExpectations(t)
}
```
In this example:

- **MockDatabase**: A mock implementation of the Database interface.

- **mock.On:** Defines the expected behavior for the GetUser method.

- **assert.Equal:** Verifies that the result matches the expected value.

This allows you to isolate the UserService and test its logic without needing a real database.

4. Test Coverage

Test coverage refers to the percentage of your codebase that is covered by unit tests. Go provides a built-in tool to measure test coverage, helping you ensure that your tests are comprehensive.

Measuring Test Coverage

To measure the test coverage, you can use the -cover flag when running your tests:

```bash

go test -cover
```

This will output the test coverage percentage for your code. You can also generate a more detailed coverage report with the following command:

```bash

go test -coverprofile=coverage.out
go tool cover -html=coverage.out
```

This generates an HTML report showing which lines of code are covered by tests and which are not.

Tools and Setup

Before diving into the hands-on examples, ensure that your environment is set up correctly for writing and running unit tests in Go.

Step 1: Installing Go

Ensure you have Go installed by running the following command:

bash

```
go version
```

If you don't have Go installed, follow the installation instructions for your operating system from the official Go website.

Step 2: Installing Testing Libraries

While Go's standard library provides excellent support for testing, you may want to install external libraries for mocking and assertion. Here's how to install **Testify**:

bash

```
go get github.com/stretchr/testify
```

Step 3: Running Tests

You can run all tests in your Go module with the following command:

bash

```
go test
```

To run tests in a specific file, use:

bash

```
go test <file-name>
```

Hands-on Examples & Projects

Building a User Authentication Module

Now that you have an understanding of how to write unit tests, let's apply this knowledge by building and testing a **User Authentication Module**.

Step 1: Define the Authentication Logic

First, let's create a basic Authenticate function that validates a user's credentials.

```go
package auth

import "errors"

type User struct {
    Username string
    Password string
}

var users = []User{
    {Username: "john", Password:
"password123"},
    {Username: "jane", Password: "qwerty"},
}

func Authenticate(username, password string)
(bool, error) {
    for _, user := range users {
        if user.Username == username &&
user.Password == password {
```

```
        return true, nil
    }
}
return false, errors.New("invalid
credentials")
}
```

Step 2: Write Tests for the Authentication Logic

Next, let's write unit tests for the Authenticate function.

```go
package auth

import "testing"

func TestAuthenticate(t *testing.T) {
    tests := []struct {
        username string
        password string
        expected bool
        err      error
    }{
        {"john", "password123", true, nil},
        {"jane", "qwerty", true, nil},
        {"john", "wrongpassword", false,
errors.New("invalid credentials")},
    }

    for _, test := range tests {
        result, err :=
Authenticate(test.username, test.password)
        if result != test.expected || err !=
nil && err.Error() != test.err.Error() {
            t.Errorf("Authenticate(%s, %s) =
%v, %v; expected %v, %v", test.username,
```

```
test.password, result, err, test.expected,
test.err)
        }
    }
}
```

This test verifies that the Authenticate function works as expected for multiple test cases.

Advanced Techniques & Optimization

Advanced Techniques for Writing Tests

- **Table-Driven Tests**: In Go, you can use table-driven tests to reduce repetition and cover a wide range of inputs.

- **Integration Testing**: While unit tests focus on individual components, integration tests check how well multiple components work together.

- **Parallel Testing**: For large applications, running tests in parallel can significantly speed up the testing process.

Troubleshooting and Problem-Solving

Common Challenges with Unit Testing in Go

- **Test Dependencies**: When unit tests rely on external systems, such as a database or an API, they can become slow and unreliable. This can be resolved through mocking and using in-memory databases.

- **Error Handling in Tests**: Ensure that errors are correctly handled in your tests, and that any expected errors are checked against the correct error messages.

Conclusion & Next Steps

In this chapter, we explored the importance of unit testing in Go, learned how to write unit tests using the testing package, and discussed best practices for mocking and measuring test coverage. You also gained hands-on experience by building and testing a user authentication module.

Next Steps:

- Continue writing unit tests for other parts of your Go applications.

- Explore more advanced testing techniques, such as **integration testing** and **end-to-end testing**.

- Learn about **continuous integration** (CI) tools to automate the running of tests.

By incorporating unit tests into your development process, you'll improve the reliability and maintainability of your Go applications. Keep experimenting, testing, and refining your skills!

Chapter 10: Building a Real-World Web App with Go

Introduction

Web development is one of the most prominent fields in programming, and Go is an increasingly popular choice for building scalable, high-performance web applications. With its simplicity, speed, and native support for concurrency, Go is well-suited for building web servers, RESTful APIs, and microservices. If you're already familiar with Go's syntax and basic concepts, it's time to take your skills to the next level by building real-world web applications.

In this chapter, we will explore the basics of web development in Go. We'll walk through setting up a web server, creating routes, handling HTTP requests, rendering templates, and using Go's powerful tools for building modern, maintainable web apps. The focus will be on building a **Blog API** that supports essential blog functionality, such as creating, updating, deleting, and fetching blog posts.

By the end of this chapter, you'll have gained hands-on experience building a web application from the ground up, and you'll understand the core concepts and best practices for structuring a web app in Go.

Core Concepts and Theory

In this section, we'll cover the fundamental concepts of web development in Go, including how to set up a web server, handle HTTP requests, and organize routes and templates. We'll also look at how Go's net/http package is designed to make web development straightforward.

1. Introduction to Web Development in Go

Web development involves creating applications that run on a web server, communicate with clients over HTTP, and serve data (often in the form of HTML, JSON, or other formats). Go's native support for HTTP servers, simplicity, and performance make it a great choice for building web applications.

Why Choose Go for Web Development?
- **Concurrency**: Go's concurrency model (via goroutines) allows you to handle multiple client requests simultaneously, making it ideal for building scalable web servers.

- **Simplicity**: Go's syntax is minimalistic and designed to be straightforward, making it easy to build and maintain web applications.

- **Performance**: Go is a compiled language that produces fast, efficient binaries, which is crucial for high-performance web applications.

- **Strong Standard Library**: Go's net/http package provides everything you need to build a web server, handle requests, and manage routing.

2. Setting Up a Basic Web Server

In Go, the net/http package provides the necessary tools to set up a web server. The http.ListenAndServe function is used to create a server that listens on a specified port and handles incoming HTTP requests.

Basic Web Server Example

Here's a simple example of a web server that responds with a "Hello, World!" message when accessed via a browser:

```go
package main

import (
    "fmt"
    "net/http"
)

func helloHandler(w http.ResponseWriter, r *http.Request) {
    fmt.Fprintf(w, "Hello, World!")
}

func main() {
    http.HandleFunc("/", helloHandler)
    fmt.Println("Server is running on http://localhost:8080")
    err := http.ListenAndServe(":8080", nil)
    if err != nil {
        fmt.Println("Error starting server:", err)
    }
}
```

- **http.HandleFunc:** Registers a handler for a specific URL pattern. In this case, we handle requests to the root path (/).

- **http.ListenAndServe:** Starts the server and listens on the specified port (8080 in this case).

- When you run this code and navigate to http://localhost:8080 in your browser, you should see the message "Hello, World!".

Routes and Handlers

Go allows you to define multiple routes and associate them with different handlers (functions that process requests). You can use http.HandleFunc to bind specific URLs to functions that process requests for those URLs.

```go
func main() {
    http.HandleFunc("/", helloHandler)    //
Route to root handler
    http.HandleFunc("/about", aboutHandler)
// Route to about handler

    fmt.Println("Server is running on
http://localhost:8080")
    err := http.ListenAndServe(":8080", nil)
    if err != nil {
        fmt.Println("Error starting
server:", err)
    }
}
```

- **/about:** In this example, we define a route for /about, which would be handled by the aboutHandler function.

3. Creating Routes, Templates, and Handling Requests

One of the most powerful features of web applications is the ability to render HTML templates dynamically. In Go, you can use the html/template package to define and render templates.

Additionally, you can handle HTTP requests using request methods such as GET, POST, PUT, and DELETE.

Using HTML Templates

Go's html/template package allows you to create HTML templates that can be dynamically populated with data. Here's an example of how to use templates in Go:

```go

package main

import (
    "fmt"
    "html/template"
    "net/http"
)

type PageVariables struct {
    Title    string
    Message  string
}

func homePage(w http.ResponseWriter, r
*http.Request) {
    pageVariables := PageVariables{
        Title:    "Welcome to My Blog",
        Message: "Hello, Go Web
Development!",
    }

    t, err :=
template.ParseFiles("home.html")
    if err != nil {
        fmt.Println(err)
    }
```

```go
    t.Execute(w, pageVariables)
}

func main() {
    http.HandleFunc("/", homePage)
    fmt.Println("Server is running on
http://localhost:8080")
    http.ListenAndServe(":8080", nil)
}
```

In this example:

- **home.html** is an HTML file with placeholders for dynamic content:

html

```html
<!DOCTYPE html>
<html lang="en">
<head>
    <meta charset="UTF-8">
    <title>{{.Title}}</title>
</head>
<body>
    <h1>{{.Message}}</h1>
</body>
</html>
```

- The homePage function passes data (PageVariables) to the template, which then renders HTML with dynamic content.

Handling HTTP Methods

Go supports handling various HTTP methods, allowing you to perform different actions based on the method used (e.g., GET, POST, PUT, DELETE).

go

```go
package main

import (
    "fmt"
    "net/http"
)

func handlePost(w http.ResponseWriter, r
*http.Request) {
    if r.Method == http.MethodPost {
        fmt.Fprintf(w, "Post request
received")
    } else {
        fmt.Fprintf(w, "This endpoint only
accepts POST requests")
    }
}

func main() {
    http.HandleFunc("/submit", handlePost)
    fmt.Println("Server is running on
http://localhost:8080")
    http.ListenAndServe(":8080", nil)
}
```

- In this example, we handle POST requests to the /submit route and respond accordingly.

Tools and Setup

Step 1: Installing Go and Dependencies

Before you can start building a web app with Go, you need to install Go and ensure your environment is properly set up.

1. **Download and Install Go**: Go to the official Go website and download the installer for your operating system. Follow the installation instructions to install Go.

2. **Setting Up Your Go Workspace**: Once Go is installed, set up your workspace:

    o The default workspace is $HOME/go, but you can customize it using the GOPATH environment variable.

    o Create a Go module in your project directory by running go mod init <module-name>.

3. **Using Go Modules**: Go modules help manage dependencies in your project. Run go mod init <module-name> to create a go.mod file in your project, which will keep track of dependencies.

Step 2: Setting Up the Project Structure

A good Go project structure is key to scalability and maintainability. For this web app, we'll use the following structure:

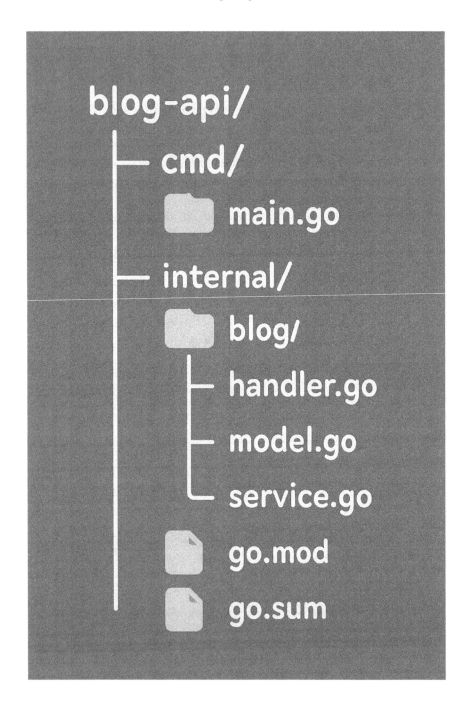

- **cmd/server**: Contains the entry point to start the server.

- **internal/blog**: Contains the core logic of the blog API (handlers, models, services).

- **go.mod and go.sum**: Manage dependencies.

Step 3: Creating the Basic Web Server

Use the code snippets from the previous section to set up a basic server that will serve as the foundation of your blog API. Ensure that your server listens on a specific port (e.g., 8080) and is capable of handling requests for creating and fetching blog posts.

Hands-on Examples & Projects

Building a Blog API

Now that you understand the basics of Go web development, let's build a **Blog API** that allows users to:

- View a list of blog posts.

- Create new blog posts.

- Edit and delete blog posts.

Step 1: Define the Blog Post Model

Create a model.go file inside the internal/blog directory to define the structure of a blog post.

go

```go
// internal/blog/model.go
package blog

type BlogPost struct {
    ID      int     `json:"id"`
    Title   string  `json:"title"`
    Content string  `json:"content"`
}
```

Step 2: Implement Blog Post Service Logic

Now, create a service.go file that contains logic to handle creating, fetching, and deleting blog posts.

go

```go
// internal/blog/service.go
package blog

var posts []BlogPost
var idCounter = 1

func CreateBlogPost(title, content string)
BlogPost {
    post := BlogPost{
        ID:      idCounter,
        Title:   title,
        Content: content,
    }
    posts = append(posts, post)
    idCounter++
    return post
}

func GetAllBlogPosts() []BlogPost {
    return posts
}
```

Step 3: Implement Blog Post Handlers

Create a handler.go file that will define HTTP handlers for your blog API endpoints.

```go
// internal/blog/handler.go
package blog

import (
    "encoding/json"
    "fmt"
    "net/http"
)

func GetPostsHandler(w http.ResponseWriter,
r *http.Request) {
    posts := GetAllBlogPosts()
    json.NewEncoder(w).Encode(posts)
}

func CreatePostHandler(w
http.ResponseWriter, r *http.Request) {
    var post BlogPost
    err :=
json.NewDecoder(r.Body).Decode(&post)
    if err != nil {
        http.Error(w, "Invalid input",
http.StatusBadRequest)
        return
    }
    createdPost :=
CreateBlogPost(post.Title, post.Content)
    w.WriteHeader(http.StatusCreated)
    json.NewEncoder(w).Encode(createdPost)
}
```

Step 4: Start the Web Server

Now, create the main server file (main.go) to start the web server and bind the routes.

go

```go
// cmd/server/main.go
package main

import (
    "fmt"
    "net/http"
    "my-go-project/internal/blog"
)

func main() {
    http.HandleFunc("/posts",
blog.GetPostsHandler)
    http.HandleFunc("/create",
blog.CreatePostHandler)

    fmt.Println("Starting server on
http://localhost:8080")
    http.ListenAndServe(":8080", nil)
}
```

Step 5: Test the Blog API

To test your API, you can use a tool like **Postman** or **cURL** to send POST and GET requests to the /posts and /create endpoints.

For example, to fetch all posts:

bash

```bash
curl http://localhost:8080/posts
```

To create a new post:

```bash
curl -X POST -d '{"title":"My First Post",
"content":"This is the content of my first
post."}' -H "Content-Type: application/json"
http://localhost:8080/create
```

Advanced Techniques & Optimization

1. Implementing Middleware

Middleware allows you to intercept HTTP requests before they reach your handler. You can use middleware for tasks like logging, authentication, and validation.

```go
func loggingMiddleware(next http.Handler)
http.Handler {
    return http.HandlerFunc(func(w
http.ResponseWriter, r *http.Request) {
        fmt.Println("Request received:",
r.Method, r.URL)
        next.ServeHTTP(w, r)
    })
}

func main() {
    http.HandleFunc("/posts",
blog.GetPostsHandler)
    http.HandleFunc("/create",
blog.CreatePostHandler)

    http.Handle("/",
loggingMiddleware(http.DefaultServeMux))
```

```
    fmt.Println("Server is running on
http://localhost:8080")
    http.ListenAndServe(":8080", nil)
}
```

2. Database Integration

For a more robust solution, integrate a database (e.g., PostgreSQL or MySQL) to store blog posts persistently instead of keeping them in memory.

Troubleshooting and Problem-Solving

Common Issues in Web Development with Go

- **Incorrect JSON Parsing**: If the JSON structure is not correctly parsed, ensure the struct tags match the JSON field names.

- **Server Not Starting**: Check if the port is already in use, or if there are issues with the ListenAndServe function.

- **Missing Routes**: If a route is not found, ensure that it's correctly registered using http.HandleFunc.

Conclusion & Next Steps

In this chapter, you learned how to build a real-world web application using Go. You covered topics like setting up a basic web server, creating routes and templates, and handling HTTP requests. You also built a **Blog API**, where users can create and fetch blog posts.

Next steps:

- Experiment with **CRUD operations** (Create, Read, Update, Delete) for a more complete API.

- Integrate a **database** to persist your blog posts.

- Learn about **authentication** and **authorization** for securing your web applications.

Keep building and experimenting, and soon you'll be able to create scalable and efficient web applications with Go!

Chapter 11: Best Practices for Efficient Go Development

Introduction

Go is renowned for its simplicity, concurrency model, and high-performance capabilities, making it a preferred language for building scalable and efficient systems. As developers, writing efficient, maintainable, and readable code is crucial for producing software that performs well in production environments, scales with ease, and remains easy to maintain and extend.

In this chapter, we will explore some of the best practices that every Go developer should know for writing efficient code. This includes understanding performance optimization, memory management, and Go's garbage collection system. Additionally, we will focus on writing clean, readable, and maintainable code—a key aspect of professional software development.

The chapter will be broken down into several sections, each focusing on an important topic for improving the efficiency and quality of your Go code. These practices will help you optimize both the runtime performance of your applications and their long-term maintainability. We'll also walk through a hands-on exercise where we refactor and improve the performance of a web application.

By the end of this chapter, you will have a comprehensive understanding of how to optimize Go code for performance, handle memory management effectively, and ensure your code is clean and maintainable.

Core Concepts and Theory

In this section, we will explore the core concepts and best practices related to performance optimization, memory management, garbage collection, and writing clean, readable code in Go. Each of these concepts is essential for writing efficient Go applications.

1. Optimizing Go Code for Performance

Performance optimization is a crucial aspect of software development, especially when you are working with large-scale applications. Go provides several mechanisms to help you write high-performance code.

Concurrency and Goroutines

Go's **goroutines** are lightweight threads managed by the Go runtime. Goroutines enable concurrent execution of tasks, which is ideal for I/O-bound operations, parallel computation, and building highly scalable systems.

To launch a goroutine, use the go keyword:

```
go
```

```
go myFunction()
```
This will execute myFunction concurrently with the rest of the program. However, goroutines must be synchronized using channels or other synchronization methods to avoid data races.

Benchmarking in Go

Before optimizing any code, it's important to understand its performance characteristics. Go includes the testing package with support for benchmarks. Here's how to benchmark a simple function:

```go
package main

import (
    "testing"
)

func add(a, b int) int {
    return a + b
}

func BenchmarkAdd(b *testing.B) {
    for i := 0; i < b.N; i++ {
        add(1, 2)
    }
}
```

Run the benchmark with the following command:

```bash
go test -bench .
```

This will measure the performance of the add function.

Optimizing Data Structures

Choosing the right data structure is crucial for performance. For example:

- **Maps** are efficient for lookups but come with overhead when the size grows large.

- **Slices** are great for dynamically sized collections but can incur performance penalties when resizing frequently.

Always consider the time complexity of operations on data structures. For example, inserting into a slice takes O(n) in the worst case if it needs to be resized, but appending to a slice is O(1) on average.

Avoiding Unnecessary Memory Allocations

Allocating memory is a relatively expensive operation, so avoid unnecessary allocations. For example, reusing buffers instead of creating new ones can improve performance.

```go
var buffer []byte

// Instead of allocating a new buffer each
time
buffer = append(buffer, []byte("new
data")...)
```

2. Memory Management and Garbage Collection

Go's memory management is largely handled by its **garbage collector (GC)**, which automatically reclaims unused memory. However, understanding how Go's memory system works and using it efficiently can help optimize your program's performance.

How Garbage Collection Works

Go's garbage collector uses a **tracing GC** approach, where it marks live objects and sweeps through memory to free up unused ones. The goal is to balance between throughput and pause times, with a focus on minimizing pauses during GC cycles.

While Go handles most memory management automatically, there are still things you can do to make memory management more efficient.

Reducing Allocations

Excessive memory allocations can put a strain on Go's garbage collector, leading to increased CPU usage and GC pauses. Minimizing unnecessary allocations is key to writing efficient Go code.

For example, avoid repeatedly creating new slices or maps in loops. Instead, preallocate slices or use buffers:

```go
// Preallocate memory
buffer := make([]byte, 0, 1024)
```

Memory Leaks in Go

Go's garbage collector is efficient at cleaning up unused memory, but it can't handle **memory leaks** caused by references that persist unexpectedly. For example, if you accidentally store references to large objects in global variables or long-lived data structures, they won't be collected by the garbage collector.

Use Go's built-in memory profiling tools to detect and fix memory leaks.

```bash
go test -memprofile mem.out
```

This will generate a memory profile that you can analyze to find memory leaks and optimize memory usage.

3. Writing Clean, Readable, and Maintainable Code

Writing clean, readable, and maintainable code is essential in Go, just as it is in any other programming language. In this section, we'll cover best practices for writing Go code that is easy to read, modify, and extend.

Consistency in Naming Conventions

Go has strict conventions for naming functions, variables, and types. Adhering to these conventions improves code readability and makes it easier for others to work with your code.

- **Variables and functions**: Use lowercase for variable and function names unless the function or variable is meant to be exported. For example: doSomething(), calculateTotal().

- **Types and constants**: Use uppercase for exported types and constants. For example: Person, MaxCount.

Commenting Your Code

Good comments explain the "why" behind your code rather than the "what." Instead of stating what the code is doing, focus on the reasoning behind it.

```go
// CalculateTotal computes the sum of all
items in the cart
func CalculateTotal(cart []Item) float64 {
    total := 0.0
    for _, item := range cart {
        total += item.Price
    }
    return total
}
```

- Avoid obvious comments like // adds two numbers.

- Use comments for complex logic or decisions that might not be immediately clear to others.

Separation of Concerns

In Go, it's important to follow the principle of **separation of concerns**, meaning that each function, package, or module should have one responsibility.

For example, a function that retrieves a user's data should only handle that task and not also be responsible for sending emails or formatting output.

Error Handling

Go does not use exceptions for error handling. Instead, errors are returned as values from functions, and it's up to the caller to handle them appropriately. Ensure that you handle errors at every stage of your application:

```go
if err != nil {
    log.Fatal(err)
}
```
Always check for errors and handle them explicitly.

Refactoring and Modularity

Refactor your code regularly to improve readability and reduce duplication. Break your code into **small, focused functions** that can be easily tested and maintained.

Tools and Setup

Before diving into hands-on examples, let's ensure you have the necessary tools set up to develop Go applications efficiently.

Step 1: Installing Go

1. Download and install Go from the official Go website.

2. Set up your Go workspace by configuring the GOPATH environment variable.

Step 2: Setting Up Your Development Environment

1. **IDE/Editor**: Use **GoLand**, **VSCode**, or **Sublime Text** for efficient development.

   o **VSCode** has excellent Go support through the Go extension, providing features like IntelliSense, debugging, and testing.

2. **Install Go Modules**: Initialize your project as a Go module with:

```bash
go mod init <module-name>
```

3. **Testing Framework**: Go's built-in testing package is sufficient for most cases. However, you can also install third-party packages like **Testify** or **GoMock** for enhanced testing capabilities.

Hands-on Examples & Projects

Refactoring and Improving Performance in Your Web App

Now that you've learned the core concepts, it's time to apply them. In this section, we'll walk through a web application refactor to improve both its performance and code quality.

Step 1: Refactoring Code for Performance

Let's start by optimizing a web server that fetches data from an external API.

```go
package main

import (
    "encoding/json"
    "fmt"
    "net/http"
    "time"
)

func fetchData(url string) ([]byte, error) {
    resp, err := http.Get(url)
    if err != nil {
        return nil, err
    }
    defer resp.Body.Close()
    return ioutil.ReadAll(resp.Body)
}

func main() {
    url :=
"https://jsonplaceholder.typicode.com/posts"
    data, err := fetchData(url)
```

```go
    if err != nil {
        fmt.Println("Error fetching data:",
err)
        return
    }
    var posts []Post
    json.Unmarshal(data, &posts)
    fmt.Println("Fetched data:", posts)
}
```

Optimizing for Concurrency

Let's optimize the web server by adding concurrency with
goroutines. This will allow the server to handle multiple
requests in parallel, improving performance under load.

```go
package main

import (
    "encoding/json"
    "fmt"
    "net/http"
    "sync"
)

func fetchData(url string, wg
*sync.WaitGroup, result chan<- []Post) {
    defer wg.Done()
    resp, err := http.Get(url)
    if err != nil {
        fmt.Println("Error fetching data:",
err)
        return
    }
    defer resp.Body.Close()
    data, _ := ioutil.ReadAll(resp.Body)
```

```
    var posts []Post
    json.Unmarshal(data, &posts)
    result <- posts
}

func main() {
    var wg sync.WaitGroup
    result := make(chan []Post)

    urls := []string{

"https://jsonplaceholder.typicode.com/posts/
1",

"https://jsonplaceholder.typicode.com/posts/
2",
    }

    for _, url := range urls {
        wg.Add(1)
        go fetchData(url, &wg, result)
    }

    go func() {
        wg.Wait()
        close(result)
    }()

    for posts := range result {
        fmt.Println(posts)
    }
}
```

This code uses goroutines to fetch data concurrently, reducing the time taken to fetch multiple API endpoints.

Advanced Techniques & Optimization

1. Advanced Performance Optimization

- **Memory Pools**: Use memory pools for large objects to minimize memory allocation overhead.

- **Zero-Cost Abstractions**: Go allows you to create abstractions without sacrificing performance, as the language focuses on producing efficient, compiled code.

2. Best Practices for Performance

- **Avoid Locks in Hot Code Paths**: Use goroutines and channels for concurrency rather than locks when possible.

- **Profiling**: Use Go's built-in profiling tools to identify bottlenecks.

Troubleshooting and Problem-Solving

Common Performance Issues

- **Excessive Memory Allocations**: Use Go's -memprofile flag to profile memory usage and avoid frequent allocations.

- **Slow Garbage Collection**: Use **manual garbage collection** tuning to optimize pause times.

- **Concurrency Bugs**: Use **race detectors** and **mutexes** to avoid race conditions in concurrent code.

Conclusion & Next Steps

In this chapter, we covered the best practices for optimizing Go code for performance, managing memory effectively, and ensuring that your code remains clean and maintainable. You learned how to benchmark and refactor code for performance, optimize memory usage, and apply concurrency for faster execution.

Next steps:

- Continue applying the practices you've learned to larger projects.

- Experiment with **Go's profiling tools** to dive deeper into performance analysis.

- Learn more about **Go's memory model** and how to optimize memory management for large-scale applications.

With the skills you've gained in this chapter, you're well-equipped to write high-performance, clean, and maintainable Go code. Happy coding!

Chapter 12: Scaling Your Go Applications

Introduction

In the world of web development and software engineering, scalability is a critical consideration. Scalability ensures that your application can handle increasing loads—whether it's more users, larger amounts of data, or an expanding set of features— without compromising performance or stability. Go, with its emphasis on simplicity, concurrency, and performance, is particularly well-suited for building scalable applications.

In this chapter, we will explore how Go handles scalability at various levels. We will start by understanding the foundational concepts of scalability, including the role of **goroutines** and **concurrency** in Go. We will then dive into strategies for **load balancing** and managing **multiple services**, two essential components for scaling applications in real-world scenarios.

Through a hands-on exercise, we will also show you how to scale a basic **Blog API**—the same API we built in previous chapters—to handle larger traffic efficiently. We will demonstrate practical strategies such as using goroutines for parallelism, optimizing resource usage, and managing multiple instances of your service.

By the end of this chapter, you will have a solid understanding of how to scale Go applications and handle large volumes of traffic while maintaining performance and reliability.

Core Concepts and Theory

1. How Go Handles Scalability

Go was designed with scalability in mind, particularly for building highly concurrent systems. At its core, Go's support for **goroutines** and its **channel-based concurrency model** make it a powerful tool for handling concurrent tasks.

Concurrency in Go: Goroutines and Channels

Go makes concurrency simpler with the use of **goroutines**, lightweight threads managed by the Go runtime. Unlike threads in other languages, which can be memory-intensive and slow to create, goroutines are lightweight, with very little overhead, enabling you to easily run hundreds of thousands or even millions of them in a Go application.

Goroutines are executed concurrently but may not run in parallel. The Go runtime schedules these goroutines on available CPU threads in a way that maximizes efficiency.

To start a goroutine, simply prefix a function call with the go keyword:

```go
go
```

```go
go myFunction()  // Runs concurrently
```

Channels are the primary mechanism for goroutines to communicate with each other. A channel allows data to be safely passed between goroutines, avoiding the need for complex locking mechanisms.

```go
go
```

```go
ch := make(chan int)
go func() {
    ch <- 1  // Send data to the channel
```

```
} ()
data := <-ch  // Receive data from the
channel
```

Goroutines and channels together form the backbone of Go's concurrency model. This model is crucial when building scalable applications, as it allows you to handle multiple tasks at once without blocking the main execution flow.

Scaling with Goroutines

To understand how goroutines improve scalability, consider an API that processes multiple requests. If each request were handled sequentially, the server would become bottlenecked. But by processing each request in its own goroutine, Go can handle many requests concurrently.

```go
go

func handleRequest(w http.ResponseWriter, r
*http.Request) {
    go processRequest(r)  // Run each
request in its own goroutine
    w.Write([]byte("Request is being
processed"))
}
```

Each time a request comes in, Go schedules the processing in a new goroutine, allowing the server to continue accepting other requests while it processes the current ones.

2. Using Goroutines for Parallelism

Parallelism differs from concurrency in that parallelism involves running multiple tasks at the same time. Go allows you to achieve parallelism through goroutines combined with multi-core processors.

Parallelizing Computational Tasks

If you have a CPU-bound task, such as an intensive computation or large dataset processing, goroutines can be used to parallelize the task across multiple CPU cores.

go

```
func compute(data []int, start, end int, ch
chan int) {
    sum := 0
    for i := start; i < end; i++ {
        sum += data[i]
    }
    ch <- sum
}

func main() {
    data := make([]int, 1000000)
    ch := make(chan int, 2)

    go compute(data, 0, len(data)/2, ch)
    go compute(data, len(data)/2, len(data),
ch)

    sum1 := <-ch
    sum2 := <-ch
    total := sum1 + sum2
    fmt.Println("Total sum:", total)
}
```

In this example, the dataset is split into two halves, each of which is processed in its own goroutine. This parallelism ensures that both halves are processed at the same time, improving performance.

Load Balancing and Managing Multiple Services

When scaling Go applications to handle large amounts of traffic, you often need to deploy multiple instances of your service and distribute traffic evenly between them. **Load balancing** is the technique used to distribute client requests across several servers or instances.

Types of Load Balancing

1. **Round-Robin Load Balancing:** This is the simplest form of load balancing. Requests are sent in a cyclic manner to each server in the pool.

2. **Least-Connections Load Balancing:** In this method, the load balancer routes requests to the server with the fewest active connections.

3. **IP Hashing:** The client's IP address is hashed to determine which server will handle the request. This method ensures that a specific client always connects to the same server.

Hands-On Exercise: Scaling Your Blog API to Handle Traffic

In this exercise, we'll scale the Blog API we built in earlier chapters to handle higher traffic. We will implement parallel processing for fetching and storing blog posts, optimize performance, and load balance multiple instances of the API.

Step 1: Refactor Blog API for Concurrent Processing

To begin scaling, we will refactor our Blog API to use goroutines for handling blog post creation and retrieval concurrently.

go

```
package main

import (
    "fmt"
    "net/http"
    "sync"
)

var posts []string

func createPostHandler(w
http.ResponseWriter, r *http.Request) {
    var wg sync.WaitGroup
    post := r.URL.Query().Get("post")
    wg.Add(1)
    go func() {
        defer wg.Done()
        posts = append(posts, post)  //
Simulate saving the post
    }()
    wg.Wait()
    fmt.Fprintf(w, "Post created: %s", post)
}

func getPostsHandler(w http.ResponseWriter,
r *http.Request) {
    var wg sync.WaitGroup
    wg.Add(1)
    go func() {
        defer wg.Done()
        for _, post := range posts {
            fmt.Fprintf(w, "Post: %s\n",
post)
        }
    }()
    wg.Wait()
}
```

```
func main() {
    http.HandleFunc("/create",
createPostHandler)
    http.HandleFunc("/posts",
getPostsHandler)
    fmt.Println("Server is running on
http://localhost:8080")
    http.ListenAndServe(":8080", nil)
}
```

Here, we refactored the createPostHandler and getPostsHandler functions to run concurrently. For example, creating a post is now handled in its own goroutine, allowing other requests to be processed while the new post is being saved.

Step 2: Implementing Load Balancing

Now that we have optimized the API for concurrency, let's look at how to handle multiple instances of the API. We'll use **Nginx** as a reverse proxy to distribute traffic to multiple instances of the API.

1. **Install Nginx**: On your machine, install Nginx as the load balancer.

2. **Configure Nginx**: Update the Nginx configuration to balance the load between multiple instances of your Go app.

```
nginx

http {
    upstream go_blog_api {
        server 127.0.0.1:8081;
        server 127.0.0.1:8082;
    }
```

```
server {
    listen 80;

    location / {
        proxy_pass http://go_blog_api;
    }
}
}
```

3. **Run Multiple Go Instances**: Start your Go API on different ports, such as 8081 and 8082:

bash

```
go run main.go --port=8081
go run main.go --port=8082
```

Now, Nginx will route incoming traffic to either instance of the Go server, balancing the load between them.

Step 3: Performance Optimizations and Monitoring

To further scale your application, use **performance optimization** tools such as Go's built-in profiler to monitor and fix bottlenecks.

bash

```
go test -bench . -memprofile mem.out
go tool pprof mem.out
```

This will give you insights into memory usage and performance bottlenecks, which you can then address by optimizing specific parts of your application.

Advanced Techniques & Optimization

1. Using Distributed Systems for Scalability

When scaling beyond a single server, you may need to introduce **distributed systems.** In Go, you can achieve this through microservices or by using messaging systems like **Kafka** or **RabbitMQ** to communicate between services.

Microservices Architecture

In a microservices architecture, each part of your application runs as a separate service, communicating over HTTP or gRPC. This makes it easier to scale specific components independently.

2. Caching for Improved Performance

Implementing caching can significantly reduce load on your services by storing frequently accessed data in memory. Go has several libraries for caching, including **groupcache** and **bigcache**.

Example of Using Caching

```go
go

package main

import (
    "github.com/patrickmn/go-cache"
    "time"
)

func main() {
    c := cache.New(5*time.Minute,
10*time.Minute)
    c.Set("key", "value",
cache.DefaultExpiration)
```

```
value, found := c.Get("key")
if found {
    fmt.Println("Cache hit:", value)
}
}
```

3. Horizontal Scaling and Service Replication

Horizontal scaling involves running multiple instances of your application to distribute the load. You can achieve horizontal scaling through cloud providers, such as **AWS**, **Google Cloud**, or **Kubernetes**.

Service Replication in Kubernetes

With **Kubernetes**, you can easily deploy and scale Go applications. Define your Go service in a Deployment and scale the number of replicas:

yaml

```yaml
apiVersion: apps/v1
kind: Deployment
metadata:
  name: go-blog-api
spec:
  replicas: 3
  selector:
    matchLabels:
      app: go-blog-api
  template:
    metadata:
      labels:
        app: go-blog-api
    spec:
      containers:
        - name: go-blog-api
```

```
image: your-image
ports:
   - containerPort: 8080
```

Kubernetes will automatically handle load balancing and replication across multiple nodes.

Troubleshooting and Problem-Solving

Common Issues When Scaling Go Applications

1. **Race Conditions**: When scaling applications, race conditions can arise due to multiple goroutines accessing shared memory. Use Go's -race flag to detect and fix these issues.

2. **Memory Leaks**: Monitor memory usage using Go's memory profiling tools. Memory leaks can occur if references to objects are not cleaned up, even after they are no longer in use.

3. **Concurrency Bottlenecks**: Too many goroutines may lead to contention over resources. Use profiling tools to identify these issues and refactor your code to minimize unnecessary goroutines.

Conclusion & Next Steps

In this chapter, we covered the critical concepts for scaling Go applications. From goroutines and concurrency to load balancing and distributed systems, you now understand how to build applications that can handle high traffic and perform efficiently under load.

Next Steps:

- Experiment with **Kubernetes** for container orchestration and **horizontal scaling** of your Go services.

- Explore advanced **caching strategies** to reduce load on your backend services.

- Study **microservices architecture** for breaking down large applications into manageable components.

With these tools and techniques, you're now well-equipped to build scalable and high-performance applications in Go. Keep experimenting with different strategies, and continue to refine your knowledge of Go's powerful concurrency model and scalability features.

Chapter 13: Deploying Go Apps

Introduction

Deploying applications is one of the most important steps in the software development lifecycle. It involves taking the code you've worked on, tested, and refined, and making it available to end users. However, deploying Go applications, like any other application, requires careful planning and preparation to ensure it runs smoothly in production.

This chapter will guide you through the process of deploying Go applications, from preparing your code for production environments to using containerization and setting up automated deployment pipelines. We will also cover essential concepts like Docker for containerizing Go apps and implementing Continuous Integration and Continuous Deployment (CI/CD) for seamless automation.

We'll end with a hands-on exercise where we'll take the **Blog API** we built in previous chapters and deploy it on **AWS**. This will give you real-world experience in deploying a Go app from start to finish.

Core Concepts and Theory

Before we dive into the practical examples, let's understand the foundational concepts that will help you deploy Go applications efficiently.

1. How to Prepare Go Apps for Production

In production environments, applications need to be robust, secure, and performant. Below are some critical steps to follow when preparing your Go application for deployment.

1.1 Building a Release Version of Your Go App

The first step in preparing your Go application for production is to build the release version of the application. Go provides a simple way to build static binaries that can be easily deployed to any system without requiring any external dependencies.

To build a release binary, you can use the go build command. Here's how to do it:

```bash

go build -o myapp
```

This will compile your Go code into a binary executable named myapp, which can be easily transferred and executed on any server.

1.2 Setting Build Flags for Production

When preparing a Go application for production, you might want to set some specific build flags to optimize the application. One common practice is to set the GOOS and GOARCH flags to ensure that the binary is built for the correct operating system and architecture.

For example, to build a binary for Linux on an AMD64 architecture:

```bash

GOOS=linux GOARCH=amd64 go build -o myapp
```

This allows you to build the Go application on a different operating system or architecture than the one on which the app will be deployed.

1.3 Dependency Management with Go Modules

Go uses a dependency management system called **Go Modules**. It ensures that your Go application has the correct versions of external libraries when it is deployed. To prepare for production, ensure you have the latest dependencies locked in your go.mod and go.sum files.

To ensure all your dependencies are correctly installed and up to date, run:

bash

```
go mod tidy
```
This will remove any unnecessary dependencies and add missing ones.

2. Using Docker to Containerize Your Go Application

Docker has become the standard tool for packaging and deploying applications in isolated environments called containers. Containers are lightweight, portable, and allow your application to run consistently across different environments.

2.1 Why Containerize Your Go App?

Containerizing your Go application provides several benefits:

- **Portability**: Docker containers ensure that your application will run consistently across different environments, whether it's on your local machine, a testing server, or in production.

- **Isolation:** Containers provide a level of isolation, ensuring that the application's dependencies, environment variables, and runtime configurations are all bundled together.

- **Scalability:** Docker makes it easy to scale your application by spinning up multiple containers or instances of your app.

2.2 Dockerizing a Go Application

To containerize a Go application, you need a Dockerfile, which contains all the instructions to build and run the container. Here's an example Dockerfile for a Go application:

```dockerfile
# Step 1: Use a base image with Go installed
FROM golang:1.16-alpine as builder

# Step 2: Set the working directory
WORKDIR /app

# Step 3:  the Go module files and install
dependencies
 go.mod go.sum ./
RUN go mod download

# Step 4:  the Go source code into the
container
  . .

# Step 5: Build the Go application
RUN go build -o myapp

# Step 6: Use a smaller base image for the
final container
FROM alpine:latest
```

```
# Step 7:  the binary from the builder
container
 --from=builder /app/myapp
/usr/local/bin/myapp

# Step 8: Run the binary when the container
starts
CMD ["myapp"]
```

Here's a breakdown of the steps:

- We use golang:1.16-alpine as the base image for the build stage because it has the Go compiler installed.

- We the go.mod and go.sum files to install the necessary dependencies.

- After the dependencies are installed, we the rest of the source code into the container and build the Go binary.

- We then use a smaller alpine base image to create a more lightweight final container.

- Finally, we set the **CMD** to run the built Go binary.

To build the Docker image, run:

```bash
```

```bash
docker build -t myapp .
```

And to run the container:

```bash
```

```bash
docker run -p 8080:8080 myapp
```

Now, your Go application is containerized and ready for deployment.

3. Continuous Integration and Continuous Deployment (CI/CD) for Go

CI/CD is the practice of automatically building, testing, and deploying your code whenever changes are made. It improves the development process by automating repetitive tasks and ensuring that code is deployed reliably.

3.1 Setting Up Continuous Integration

To set up CI for a Go project, we will use **GitHub Actions**, which is a CI/CD platform integrated with GitHub. First, create a .github/workflows/ci.yml file with the following configuration:

```yaml
yaml

name: Go CI

on:
  push:
    branches:
      - main
  pull_request:
    branches:
      - main

jobs:
  build:
    runs-on: ubuntu-latest

    steps:
    - uses: actions/checkout@v2
    - name: Set up Go
      uses: actions/setup-go@v2
      with:
        go-version: '1.16'
    - name: Install dependencies
```

```
    run: go mod tidy
  - name: Run tests
    run: go test -v ./...
```

This configuration sets up a GitHub Action that:

- Triggers on pushes to the main branch or pull requests targeting the main branch.

- Sets up a Go environment on an Ubuntu machine.

- Installs Go dependencies with go mod tidy.

- Runs Go tests using go test.

3.2 Continuous Deployment (CD)

To automate the deployment of your Go app, you can extend your CI pipeline to include a deployment step. For example, here's how you could deploy your Dockerized Go app to **AWS Elastic Beanstalk** using GitHub Actions.

1. Set up an **Elastic Beanstalk** environment for your Go app.

2. Use AWS CLI and GitHub Actions to deploy your Docker image.

```yaml
name: Deploy to AWS Elastic Beanstalk

on:
  push:
    branches:
      - main

jobs:
  deploy:
    runs-on: ubuntu-latest
```

```
steps:
  - name: Checkout code
    uses: actions/checkout@v2
  - name: Set up AWS CLI
    uses: aws-actions/configure-aws-
credentials@v1
    with:
      aws-access-key-id: ${{
secrets.AWS_ACCESS_KEY_ID }}
      aws-secret-access-key: ${{
secrets.AWS_SECRET_ACCESS_KEY }}
      aws-region: us-west-2
  - name: Deploy to Elastic Beanstalk
    run: |
      eb init -p docker myapp --region
us-west-2
      eb create myapp-env
      eb deploy
```

In this configuration:

- **AWS credentials** are securely stored in GitHub Secrets.

- The eb CLI is used to deploy the Dockerized application to Elastic Beanstalk.

Tools and Setup

In this section, we'll discuss the tools required for deploying Go applications, setting up the environment, and configuring CI/CD pipelines.

1. Tools for Go Deployment

- **Docker:** Used for containerizing your Go application, ensuring portability and easy deployment across various environments.

- **AWS Elastic Beanstalk**: A fully managed service that helps deploy, manage, and scale web applications and services.

- **GitHub Actions**: A CI/CD platform integrated with GitHub, ideal for automating testing, building, and deployment workflows.

- **AWS CLI**: A command-line tool to interact with AWS services, including Elastic Beanstalk.

2. Setting Up the Development Environment

To set up the environment for deploying Go apps:

1. **Install Docker**: Follow the installation guide on Docker's official website.

2. **Set Up AWS Elastic Beanstalk**: If you don't have an AWS account, create one at AWS. Then, install the **AWS CLI** and set up Elastic Beanstalk by following the instructions here.

3. **Set Up GitHub Actions**: Create a GitHub repository for your Go project, and then follow the instructions above to set up GitHub Actions for CI/CD.

Hands-on Examples & Projects

Deploying Your Blog App on AWS

Let's now walk through the process of deploying our **Blog API** to AWS, starting with containerizing it, setting up a CI/CD pipeline, and deploying it using **AWS Elastic Beanstalk**.

Step 1: Dockerize the Blog API

We've already covered how to Dockerize the Blog API. Ensure your Dockerfile is set up as shown earlier. After creating the Docker image, run the following command to verify it:

```bash
```

```
docker build -t blog-api .
docker run -p 8080:8080 blog-api
```

You should be able to access the API locally at http://localhost:8080.

Step 2: Set Up AWS Elastic Beanstalk

1. Install the **AWS CLI** and **Elastic Beanstalk CLI**.

2. Initialize your Elastic Beanstalk application using the eb init command.

3. Create an environment with eb create and deploy using eb deploy.

Step 3: Setting Up CI/CD Pipeline

Follow the earlier instructions to set up a GitHub Action for automating testing, building, and deploying the application. Whenever you push changes to the main branch, the pipeline will automatically build and deploy the application to AWS.

Advanced Techniques & Optimization

1. Advanced Docker Optimization

Optimize your Dockerfiles by using multi-stage builds and minimizing the size of your images. Use the alpine version of base images to reduce the image size.

2. Advanced CI/CD Strategies

- **Blue-Green Deployment**: A deployment strategy where you have two identical environments. One environment is live, while the other is used to deploy the new version. Once the new version is tested, traffic is switched over to the new version with minimal downtime.

- **Canary Releases**: Gradually roll out changes to a small subset of users before deploying to everyone. This ensures that if an issue arises, it only affects a small number of users.

Troubleshooting and Problem-Solving

1. Common Deployment Issues

- **Incorrect AWS Permissions**: Ensure that your AWS credentials have the necessary permissions to deploy to Elastic Beanstalk.

- **Docker Image Build Failures**: Check the Dockerfile for any errors. Use docker logs to debug failed containers.

- **Deployment Failures in Elastic Beanstalk**: Review the logs using eb logs to understand the root cause of deployment issues.

Conclusion & Next Steps

In this chapter, we've covered the steps for preparing, containerizing, and deploying Go applications to production environments using Docker and AWS. We also explored the importance of CI/CD in automating the build, test, and deployment process.

Next Steps:

- Experiment with **advanced deployment strategies**, such as blue-green deployments and canary releases.

- Learn more about **scaling** your Go applications in the cloud by using **AWS Lambda** and **Kubernetes**.

By following these best practices and utilizing the tools and techniques discussed in this chapter, you're well on your way to deploying and managing Go applications at scale in real-world environments.

Chapter 14: Real-World Applications of Go

Introduction

Go, also known as Golang, has gained significant popularity over the past decade due to its simplicity, performance, and concurrency features. Initially created by Google to address scalability and performance challenges in large systems, Go has become the go-to language for various domains, including cloud services, DevOps, microservices, machine learning, and more. This chapter explores some of the most compelling real-world applications of Go and demonstrates its versatility in solving complex problems across diverse industries.

In the first part of the chapter, we'll dive into the role Go plays in **cloud services and DevOps,** where its efficiency and ease of deployment have made it a dominant player. Then, we will explore Go's role in **microservices architecture,** which has become one of the most popular architectural patterns for building scalable and maintainable systems.

We will also look at how Go is used in emerging fields like **machine learning and data science**, where its performance and concurrency features allow it to handle large datasets and complex computations efficiently. Lastly, we will explore Go's impact in **healthcare, finance, and logistics**, where it helps drive secure, high-performance systems that are critical in these data-heavy sectors.

To tie all these concepts together, we will wrap up the chapter with a **case study:** building a **payment processing system in Go,** demonstrating how Go's strengths make it the perfect language for high-volume, mission-critical systems.

Core Concepts and Theory

In this section, we will discuss the fundamental concepts that make Go such a versatile language for real-world applications. We will explore how Go handles concurrency, performance, scalability, and the features that make it ideal for cloud, microservices, and machine learning applications.

1. Go in Cloud Services and DevOps

1.1 Why Go for Cloud and DevOps?

Go has become a popular language for cloud-native applications and DevOps due to its combination of simplicity, efficiency, and support for concurrency. Cloud services require high performance and scalability, and Go excels at these requirements. Whether building APIs, microservices, or complex distributed systems, Go's features help developers build and deploy efficient applications.

1.2 Go's Role in Cloud Services

Cloud-native applications require efficient handling of multiple concurrent requests, often from different geographic locations. Go is perfect for building such applications due to its **goroutines** and **channels** for concurrency. It can also scale easily with tools like Kubernetes and Docker, which are commonly used in cloud environments.

For example, **Kubernetes**, one of the most popular container orchestration platforms, is written in Go. The Go programming language's concurrency model is essential in

Kubernetes for managing the complex processes involved in scheduling and managing containers across clusters.

1.3 Go in DevOps

In the DevOps space, Go has become a key player for automating workflows, continuous integration (CI), and continuous delivery (CD). Many of the most popular DevOps tools, such as **Docker**, **Terraform**, and **Prometheus**, are written in Go because it provides a good balance of performance and simplicity. The fact that Go compiles to a statically linked binary makes it ideal for deploying and managing infrastructure, reducing reliance on third-party dependencies, and making systems easier to maintain.

2. Go for Microservices Architecture

2.1 What Are Microservices?

Microservices architecture is an approach where a large application is divided into smaller, loosely coupled services that communicate with each other through well-defined APIs. Each microservice is designed to perform a specific function and can be developed, deployed, and scaled independently of other services. This architecture enables faster development, better scalability, and easier maintenance.

2.2 Why Use Go for Microservices?

Go's concurrency model, high performance, and easy-to-understand syntax make it an ideal language for microservices. Some of the key advantages of using Go for microservices include:

- **Concurrency and Parallelism**: Go's goroutines and channels allow developers to easily handle concurrent tasks in microservices, enabling efficient communication between different services and improving overall system performance.

- **Minimalism:** Go's simple syntax means that developers can focus on building functionality rather than dealing with complex abstractions.

- **Efficient Resource Usage:** Go applications are highly efficient and can run on minimal hardware, which is particularly useful in a microservices architecture where many services may be running simultaneously.

2.3 Example of Microservices in Go

Consider a simple e-commerce application with multiple services: product management, order processing, and payment handling. Each of these services could be implemented as a separate Go application, with each one handling specific tasks such as managing products or processing payments.

Each service can be developed and deployed independently, with Go handling the concurrency and scalability of these services:

```go
// Simple API to handle product data
(Product Service)
package main

import (
    "encoding/json"
    "fmt"
    "net/http"
)

type Product struct {
    ID      int      `json:"id"`
```

```
    Name   string `json:"name"`
    Price int    `json:"price"`
}

func getProductHandler(w
http.ResponseWriter, r *http.Request) {
    product := Product{ID: 1, Name:
"Laptop", Price: 1000}
    json.NewEncoder(w).Encode(product)
}

func main() {
    http.HandleFunc("/product",
getProductHandler)
    fmt.Println("Product service running on
http://localhost:8081")
    http.ListenAndServe(":8081", nil)
}
```
In this example, we've built a **Product Service** using Go, which could be part of a larger microservices architecture.

3. Go in Machine Learning and Data Science

3.1 Go for Data-Intensive Applications

While Go is not as well-known as Python for data science, it is increasingly being used in the field for high-performance applications that involve large datasets or complex calculations. Go's concurrency model is especially useful when working with data pipelines that need to handle multiple tasks at once, such as reading from multiple data sources, processing data, and writing results back to storage.

3.2 Libraries and Frameworks for Machine Learning in Go

Although Go doesn't have as many libraries for machine learning as Python, there are several libraries available for machine learning tasks:

- **Gorgonia**: A machine learning library that mimics the functionality of TensorFlow and PyTorch. It allows you to build and train neural networks in Go.

- **GoLearn**: A library that provides algorithms and tools for machine learning, such as classification, regression, and clustering.

3.3 Example: Building a Simple Model with Gorgonia

Here's an example of using **Gorgonia** to train a simple neural network for classification:

```go
package main

import (
    "gorgonia.org/gorgonia"
    "gorgonia.org/tensor"
)

func main() {
    g := gorgonia.NewGraph()

    // Input data and labels
    X := tensor.New(tensor.WithShape(4, 2),
tensor.WithShape(1, 4))
    Y := tensor.New(tensor.WithShape(4, 1),
tensor.WithShape(1, 4))
```

```
    // Define weights and biases
    w := gorgonia.NewTensor(g, X.Shape()[1],
gorgonia.WithShape(2, 1),
gorgonia.WithName("weights"))
    b := gorgonia.NewTensor(g, 1,
gorgonia.WithShape(1),
gorgonia.WithName("bias"))

    // Define the neural network and loss
function
    layer :=
gorgonia.Must(gorgonia.Add(gorgonia.Must(gor
gonia.Mul(X, w)), b))
    loss :=
gorgonia.Must(gorgonia.Mean(gorgonia.Must(go
rgonia.Sub(layer, Y))))

    // Forward pass and backpropagation
    gorgonia.Read(w, w)
    gorgonia.Read(b, b)
}
```

In this example, we define a simple neural network using the **Gorgonia** library, build the computation graph, and define the loss function for backpropagation.

4. Go in Healthcare, Finance, and Logistics

4.1 Healthcare Applications

In the healthcare industry, Go is used to build scalable applications for processing medical data, managing patient records, and integrating various systems. Go's concurrency model allows healthcare applications to handle multiple data sources in real-time, while its high performance ensures that large datasets can be processed quickly.

4.2 Finance Applications

Go is increasingly used in the financial sector for building applications such as high-frequency trading systems, payment processors, and banking systems. The language's speed, efficiency, and reliability make it a good fit for applications that require low latency and high throughput.

4.3 Logistics Applications

In logistics, Go is used to optimize route planning, inventory management, and supply chain tracking. With its ability to process large volumes of data concurrently, Go can help logistics companies build efficient, real-time systems.

Case Study: Building a Payment Processing System in Go

In this section, we'll walk through building a simple **payment processing system** using Go. This example will demonstrate how Go's performance and concurrency features make it ideal for handling payment transactions at scale.

1. Designing the Payment System

The payment system consists of several components:

1. **Transaction Processing**: This component handles incoming payment requests and processes them.

2. **Account Management**: Manages user accounts and their balances.

3. **Logging and Monitoring**: Logs payment activities for auditing and debugging purposes.

2. Building the Transaction Processor

```go
go

package main

import (
    "fmt"
    "log"
    "net/http"
    "sync"
)

type Transaction struct {
    ID     int     `json:"id"`
    Amount float64 `json:"amount"`
}

var balance float64 = 1000
var mu sync.Mutex

func processTransaction(w
http.ResponseWriter, r *http.Request) {
    var transaction Transaction
    if err :=
json.NewDecoder(r.Body).Decode(&transaction)
; err != nil {
        http.Error(w, err.Error(),
http.StatusBadRequest)
        return
    }

    mu.Lock()
    balance += transaction.Amount
    mu.Unlock()
```

```
    fmt.Fprintf(w, "Transaction processed.
New balance: %f", balance)
}

func main() {
    http.HandleFunc("/pay",
processTransaction)
    log.Println("Payment system running...")
    log.Fatal(http.ListenAndServe(":8080",
nil))
}
```

This simple Go application processes payment transactions and updates the user's balance concurrently. The use of **mutexes** ensures that multiple transactions do not conflict with each other.

3. Handling Transactions with Goroutines

To scale the payment processing, we can use goroutines to handle each payment request concurrently. This allows the system to handle multiple payment requests at the same time without blocking.

```go
func processTransactionConcurrently(w
http.ResponseWriter, r *http.Request) {
    var transaction Transaction
    if err :=
json.NewDecoder(r.Body).Decode(&transaction)
; err != nil {
        http.Error(w, err.Error(),
http.StatusBadRequest)
        return
    }

    go func() {
```

```
    mu.Lock()
    balance += transaction.Amount
    mu.Unlock()
  } ()

  fmt.Fprintf(w, "Transaction is being
processed")
}
```

This approach ensures that the server can continue handling requests while payment transactions are being processed in the background.

Tools and Setup

To deploy and manage Go applications in real-world use cases, you'll need several tools and platforms:

1. Development Tools

- **Go**: The programming language itself, including the Go compiler and tools like go build and go test.

- **Docker**: For containerizing Go applications, ensuring they run consistently across different environments.

- **Kubernetes**: For managing and orchestrating containerized applications in production.

- **AWS, GCP, Azure**: Cloud platforms to deploy and scale applications.

- **CI/CD Tools**: GitHub Actions, Jenkins, or CircleCI for automating testing, builds, and deployments.

2. Setting Up the Development Environment

1. Install Go from the official website: golang.org

2. Set up **Docker** to containerize your applications: Docker Install Guide

3. Set up Kubernetes or a similar orchestration tool for managing your deployments.

4. Configure a CI/CD pipeline using tools like **GitHub Actions** or **Jenkins** to automate your development workflow.

Advanced Techniques & Optimization

1. Optimizing Go for High-Performance Applications

- **Memory Management:** Use Go's memory profiling tools to monitor and optimize memory usage.

- **Concurrency Optimization:** Make use of Go's goroutines and channels to handle high-concurrency workloads efficiently.

- **Load Testing:** Use tools like **Apache JMeter** or **k6** to test your Go applications under high load and identify performance bottlenecks.

2. Implementing Scalable Microservices

- **Service Discovery:** Use tools like **Consul** or **Etcd** for service discovery in microservices architectures.

- **Resilience:** Implement patterns like **circuit breakers** and **retry logic** to handle failures in distributed systems.

Troubleshooting and Problem-Solving

1. Common Issues

- **Concurrency Bugs**: Use Go's race detector (go run -race) to identify and fix race conditions.

- **Memory Leaks**: Use Go's memory profiling tools to detect memory leaks in your application.

2. Debugging Tips

- **Logs**: Always log useful information for debugging and monitoring purposes. Tools like **logrus** and **zap** are popular for structured logging in Go.

- **Remote Debugging**: Use **Delve** for remote debugging of Go applications running in production.

Conclusion & Next Steps

In this chapter, we have explored the powerful real-world applications of Go across industries such as cloud services, microservices, machine learning, healthcare, and finance. We also demonstrated how Go can be used to build a simple payment processing system that can scale effectively using Go's concurrency features.

Next Steps:

- Deepen your understanding of **cloud-native development** with Go by building and deploying larger systems using **Kubernetes**.

- Experiment with Go's machine learning libraries to develop data-intensive applications.

- Learn more about **microservices patterns** such as service discovery, load balancing, and resilience in distributed systems.

By following the practices and strategies outlined in this chapter, you'll be well-equipped to build scalable, performant, and reliable applications with Go. Happy coding!

Conclusion

Introduction

Congratulations! If you've made it this far, you've already traveled a significant portion of your Go programming journey. Whether you are just starting to explore the world of Go or you've been using it for a while, you've now gained the knowledge and skills needed to build, deploy, and scale applications using one of the most efficient and powerful programming languages in the world today.

The journey you've embarked on by learning Go is one that can take you into many areas of software development. From building simple command-line applications to developing complex cloud-based systems, Go provides the tools and capabilities to help you succeed in numerous domains. In this final chapter, we're going to take a step back, reflect on your journey, and explore what comes next.

Learning Go is not just about mastering the syntax or understanding concurrency and data types. It's about developing a mindset and approach that allows you to tackle real-world problems with confidence. We'll cover how to continue learning and growing as a Go developer, including resources to deepen your knowledge and advance your career. Finally, we'll leave you with some final words of encouragement to help you stay motivated and empowered to build great software.

Core Concepts and Theory

In this section, we will take a deeper look at how to keep progressing as a Go developer. It's not enough to simply finish a book or tutorial; growth comes from continual learning and application. Below are several ways you can continue advancing your knowledge and experience with Go, building on the foundation we've covered throughout this guide.

1. Mastering Concurrency and Performance

One of the standout features of Go is its powerful concurrency model. If you've grasped the basics of **goroutines** and **channels**, there's still much more to explore. As you continue to write more concurrent applications, here are some areas to delve into:

1.1 Advanced Goroutine Patterns

Once you are comfortable with launching and managing goroutines, you can move on to more advanced patterns such as:

- **Worker Pools**: A common pattern for handling large volumes of tasks concurrently while limiting the number of goroutines to avoid overwhelming the system.

- **Fan-out, Fan-in**: Distributing tasks across multiple goroutines and then collecting their results in a central location.

Here's a simple example of a worker pool pattern:

```go
go

package main

import (
    "fmt"
    "sync"
)
```

```go
func worker(id int, jobs <-chan int, results
chan<- int) {
    for j := range jobs {
        fmt.Printf("Worker %d started job
%d\n", id, j)
        results <- j * 2 // Example work:
multiply by 2
        fmt.Printf("Worker %d finished job
%d\n", id, j)
    }
}

func main() {
    const numWorkers = 3
    jobs := make(chan int, 100)
    results := make(chan int, 100)

    // Start workers
    for w := 1; w <= numWorkers; w++ {
        go worker(w, jobs, results)
    }

    // Send jobs
    for j := 1; j <= 5; j++ {
        jobs <- j
    }

    close(jobs)

    // Receive results
    for a := 1; a <= 5; a++ {
        fmt.Println("Result:", <-results)
    }
}
```

1.2 Profiling and Optimizing Performance

As a Go developer, it's important to understand how to measure the performance of your applications. Go provides a built-in tool for performance profiling. By using pprof, you can measure CPU usage, memory allocation, and goroutine activity, enabling you to identify performance bottlenecks and optimize your code accordingly.

For example, you can run a CPU profile by executing:

```bash

go test -bench . -cpuprofile cpu.out
go tool pprof cpu.out
```

Using these tools, you can track down issues such as excessive memory allocations or high CPU usage and apply optimizations such as reducing unnecessary allocations or refactoring slow parts of the code.

2. Building and Deploying Real-World Applications

As you advance, applying your Go knowledge to real-world applications is the best way to solidify your learning. Here are some areas where you can go deeper:

2.1 Cloud-Native Development

Cloud-native applications are designed to run in dynamic environments like Kubernetes, leveraging containers for scalability and resilience. Go's performance and simplicity make it the perfect fit for developing cloud-native services, particularly in systems like **microservices** or **serverless architectures**.

You can start by contributing to **open-source cloud projects** or even building your own cloud-based applications, utilizing tools like **AWS Lambda, Google Cloud Functions**, and **Kubernetes**.

2.2 Building Scalable Web Applications

Building large-scale, production-ready applications in Go involves not just writing the backend logic but also thinking about how the application can scale under high loads. By learning how to integrate your Go applications with **load balancers, caching systems**, and **database replication**, you can create applications that handle high traffic and large amounts of data.

For example, building a **RESTful API** in Go can be a great next project to apply what you've learned and understand how APIs fit into the larger architecture of web applications. You can use **Gin** or **Echo**, two popular Go web frameworks, to quickly set up your API routes.

2.3 Deploying Go Applications

Deployment and infrastructure management are essential skills for modern developers. Learning how to deploy Go applications on **cloud platforms** like **AWS, Azure**, or **Google Cloud** is a critical step. The **Docker** containerization process allows you to bundle your Go application along with all its dependencies, ensuring consistency across different environments.

Tools and Setup

To keep improving as a Go developer, you need to get comfortable with a variety of tools and practices. This section will cover some of the essential tools and environments that will help you advance your Go programming skills and develop sophisticated applications.

1. Setting Up a Local Development Environment

To effectively write and deploy Go applications, having a proper local development environment is essential. Here's a quick guide to getting started:

1. **Install Go**: Download the latest version of Go from golang.org.

2. **Text Editor/IDE**: Choose a text editor or IDE that supports Go. Some popular choices include:

   o **VS Code** with the Go extension

   o **GoLand** (a JetBrains product)

   o **Vim** with Go-related plugins

3. **Version Control**: Use **Git** for version control. Setting up a GitHub or GitLab account is recommended for sharing and collaborating on projects.

4. **Docker**: Install **Docker** to create containers for your applications. This ensures that your Go apps run the same way across various environments.

5. **CI/CD Tools**: Set up continuous integration using tools like **GitHub Actions**, **Travis CI**, or **Jenkins** to automate your build, test, and deployment workflows.

2. Cloud Tools and Platforms

When your applications grow, using cloud-based tools becomes necessary:

- **AWS, Google Cloud, or Azure:** Learn how to deploy your Go applications to the cloud for better scalability and performance.

- **Kubernetes:** Use Kubernetes to orchestrate your containers and manage your microservices at scale.

- **CI/CD Pipelines:** Tools like **GitLab CI**, **Jenkins**, and **CircleCI** will help automate your deployment process, ensuring faster and more reliable releases.

Hands-on Examples & Projects

Project 1: Building a Scalable Go Web API

Now that you have a strong understanding of Go, let's put this knowledge to the test by building a scalable Go web API. The goal is to build a blog API with CRUD functionality, deploy it using Docker, and then scale it horizontally using Kubernetes.

Step 1: Building the API

Start by creating a basic Go server with API routes for managing blog posts.

```go

package main

import (
    "encoding/json"
    "fmt"
    "log"
    "net/http"
)

type Post struct {
```

```go
    ID      int     `json:"id"`
    Title string `json:"title"`
    Body  string `json:"body"`
}

var posts []Post

func createPostHandler(w
http.ResponseWriter, r *http.Request) {
    var post Post
    if err :=
json.NewDecoder(r.Body).Decode(&post); err
!= nil {
        http.Error(w, err.Error(),
http.StatusBadRequest)
        return
    }

    post.ID = len(posts) + 1
    posts = append(posts, post)
    json.NewEncoder(w).Encode(post)
}

func getPostsHandler(w http.ResponseWriter,
r *http.Request) {
    json.NewEncoder(w).Encode(posts)
}

func main() {
    http.HandleFunc("/posts",
getPostsHandler)
    http.HandleFunc("/create",
createPostHandler)
    log.Println("API is running on
http://localhost:8080")
    log.Fatal(http.ListenAndServe(":8080",
nil))
```

```
}
```

Step 2: Dockerizing the Application

Once you have the basic Go API working, it's time to Dockerize it. You can follow the Docker setup from Chapter 12, using the Dockerfile mentioned earlier. Build and run the Docker image:

```bash
docker build -t blog-api .
docker run -p 8080:8080 blog-api
```

Step 3: Scaling with Kubernetes

Next, create a Kubernetes deployment to scale your blog API horizontally. Use the following Kubernetes configuration:

```yaml
apiVersion: apps/v1
kind: Deployment
metadata:
  name: blog-api
spec:
  replicas: 3
  selector:
    matchLabels:
      app: blog-api
  template:
    metadata:
      labels:
        app: blog-api
    spec:
      containers:
      - name: blog-api
        image: blog-api:latest
        ports:
        - containerPort: 8080
```

This deployment configuration will ensure that your blog API runs on three separate instances, making it scalable and fault-tolerant.

Advanced Techniques & Optimization

1. Optimizing Go Applications

As your applications grow, performance becomes increasingly important. Here are a few techniques for optimizing your Go applications:

- **Use Profiling Tools**: Use Go's built-in profiling tools to monitor CPU, memory, and goroutine usage.

- **Benchmarking**: Use go test -bench to benchmark parts of your application and identify bottlenecks.

- **Memory Management**: Go's garbage collector is automatic, but large objects can still introduce performance issues. Use **pointers** and **value types** carefully to minimize unnecessary memory allocations.

2. Error Handling and Logging

Go's explicit error handling requires developers to be proactive. Use logging libraries like **logrus** and **zap** for structured and easy-to-read logs. For production, ensure that logs are centrally collected and monitored using tools like **Prometheus** or **Elasticsearch**.

Troubleshooting and Problem-Solving

Common Issues

- **Concurrency Bugs:** Use Go's -race flag to detect race conditions and eliminate concurrency issues.

- **Slow Performance:** Profile the application to detect memory leaks and CPU hotspots.

- **Deployment Failures:** Ensure that your Go binaries are compiled for the right OS and architecture, especially when deploying on cloud platforms.

Conclusion & Next Steps

Your Go journey doesn't end here. The skills you've developed in this book lay a solid foundation for tackling real-world problems and building scalable applications. However, there's always more to learn.

As you continue your learning journey, keep exploring Go's ecosystem, experiment with new tools, and apply your knowledge to more advanced projects. Contribute to open-source projects, collaborate with other developers, and stay up-to-date with the latest advancements in Go development.

Next Steps:

- Explore **advanced Go patterns** such as **CQRS, Event Sourcing**, and **Domain-Driven Design.**

- Dive deeper into **cloud-native development** with Go by building containerized applications and deploying them using tools like **Kubernetes.**

Remember, every line of code you write is a step toward becoming an expert in Go. Keep coding, stay curious, and most importantly, have fun building great software!

Happy coding!